LIFESTORIES

LIFESTORIES

FINDING GOD'S "VOICE OF TRUTH"
THROUGH EVERYDAY LIFE

MARK HALL

WITH TIM LUKE

provident
B O O K S

LIFESTORIES
Finding God's "Voice of Truth" Through Everyday Life
Published and Distributed by Provident Books,
a division of Provident Label Group LLC,
741 Cool Springs Blvd., Franklin, Tennessee 37067.

Visit our Web site: www.providentlabelgroup.com

Credits
Development Editor: Tim Luke
Copy Editor: Don Pape
Art Director / Cover Design: Tim Parker
Interior Designer: Rose Yancik
Production Managers: David Steffens, Michelle Pearson

Library of Congress Control Number: 2006902591

ISBN-13 978-1-55897-002-1

Printed in the United States of America
2006—First Edition

10 9 8 7 6 5 4 3 2 1

To my wife, Melanie. You are a beautiful picture of
Proverbs 31 and an example to our family, our friends,
our students, our children, and to me of what it means to be
"walking with Jesus." You are truly God's priceless gift to me.

contents

Foreword

"Give this a listen and let me know what you think."

This was all the "setup" I received when my good friend, Mark Miller, handed me a CD of a band called Casting Crowns. He would later explain that they were a band comprised of youth workers who had made a couple of their own recordings for the kids in their church youth groups. I played the CD in my car and heard something in the voice of the singer that told me these songs were coming from a deep place in his heart, and it made me listen.

Then I came to a song that really caught my attention. By the time the chorus came around and asked the question, *"If we are the body, why aren't His arms reaching?"* I was hooked. I got more excited as I heard honesty, vulnerability, and an obvious passion for the heart of God in the lyrics, with some pretty cool music accompanying them. I had to know more about this band. In particular, I needed to know who this Mark Hall guy was who was writing these songs, saying these kinds of things, and asking these kinds of questions. I remember thinking to myself, *"Man, the church and the world need to hear this."* I told Mark Miller that I'd gladly do whatever I could to help get this band and these songs heard.

Within a few months Mark Miller invited me into the process of helping produce the first Casting Crowns record and gave me a copy of some new song ideas that Mark Hall was working on for the band.

I popped the CD into the player in my car and listened through some of the very "rough" ideas that this youth pastor was working on. As a writer, I could appreciate the raw form these song demos were in as Mark fumbled his way through the chords on the piano and sang some of the lyrics laced with the occasional "la, la" where words would eventually go. Again, I found myself really drawn into the honesty and passion of the lyrics. I felt like Mark was opening up his journal and letting me travel along with him on his journey of faith, stopping for moments along the way to look up into the face of Jesus and get an eternal perspective. This resonated so much with me as a fellow songwriter and a fellow "pilgrim on the journey," because this is what I've always hoped my songs would feel like to my own listeners.

One of the unique aspects of Mark's songs that has endeared so many people to the music of Casting Crowns is his ability to make you feel like you're listening to the heart of a good friend. He can ask you tough questions and you're not offended because you know he's wrestling with the same questions. He can challenge you because you sense that he's simply inviting you into the place where he also has been challenged. He can offer you encouragement, and you know it's coming from a place of hurt and hope that has been lived and not just imagined for the purpose of writing a song. You never feel like you're getting "preached at," and yet his songs contain some of the most profound sermons. These are not just the marks of a great songwriter, but a great friend.

No doubt, the songs of Mark Hall and the music of Casting Crowns have impacted the lives of millions. I've enjoyed the privilege of touring with them and have seen the tears streaming down the faces of many people in the audience as they sing along with *Voice of Truth*. And I believe this song title probably captures—as well as any could—the reason why Casting Crowns' music has and will continue to have its great impact. It is only God's voice speaking and breathing truth into our lives that gives us anything of value to share with others.

I'm so thankful that God has entrusted a good gift to Mark Hall. Obviously you're reading this book because God has used that gift in your life at some level and has spoken to you through the songs of Mark Hall and Casting Crowns.

I know it is Mark's hope and prayer, as it is mine, that as you read the stories, meet some of the people, and learn about the inspiration behind many of Mark's songs, you will see yourself in the story and listen for the "Voice of Truth" speaking into your life in a fresh way. And may you let your *Lifesong* sing back to Him. God bless you, and enjoy!

Steven Curtis Chapman
March, 2006

Personal Note

For this reason, because I have heard of your faith in
the Lord Jesus and your love toward all the saints,
I do not cease to give thanks for you, remembering you
in my prayers, that the God of our Lord Jesus Christ,
the Father of glory, may give you a spirit of wisdom
and of revelation in the knowledge of him, having the
eyes of your hearts enlightened, that you may know
what is the hope to which he has called you, what are
the riches of his glorious inheritance in the saints, and
what is the immeasurable greatness of his power
toward us who believe...

EPHESIANS 1:15-19

SOUND CHECK

My sincere prayer is that you will not simply read this book but experience it. Furthest from my mind is the notion of entertaining you. It is not enough merely to skim over pages, especially when they include God's Word. While the Lord most certainly does not need this paltry book or any of man's efforts, He can use such tools to deepen our faith, reveal more of Himself, illumine our minds, and inspire our hearts.

I ask you first to pray for God to somehow speak to you through the Scriptures included in these chapters. Each chapter was prayed over as it was written—and invariably the prayer asked God to use this book to exalt the name of Jesus Christ. I prayed in so many words that He would use this work to help lead people to His Word, and to Him, so that He could encourage them, inspire them, instruct them, motivate them—and, if need be, convict and correct. I prayed for Him to save souls. To change lives.

Next, I encourage you to take time to mull over the questions in *The Bottom Line* section that closes each chapter. Please don't give these questions short shrift. Seriously ask the Lord to help you answer them truthfully, and then grab your journal—or start one—and record your answers.

Finally, I encourage you to complete the exercises in the last two sections of the book and write your responses on the lines provided. *My Lifesong* offers a chance to record your personal testimony (chances are you have never committed it to paper; you'll be astounded at how God uses this exercise and the memories He raises). The final section is entitled *Next Stanza*, which is an opportunity to record your hopes and dreams and where you believe the Lord is taking you.

God has the most room to work in expectant hearts. Anytime you enter into a study that includes God's Word, ask Him to teach you, and then believe He will. Let Him have His way, whatever that may mean for your life. He longs to write a beautiful lifestory for you. And what better Author is there than the Word become flesh?

Testimony

But he said to me, "My grace is sufficient for you,
for my power is made perfect in weakness." Therefore I
will boast all the more gladly of my weaknesses,
so that the power of Christ may rest upon me.
2 CORINTHIANS 12:9

FOUR CHORDS

The sunlight filtered through the stained glass windows in the historic chapel, shading the room in all the subtleties of blue, the color of my life.

I sat down on the back row and exhaled. The bottom could not have fallen out of my first day at college, the first day of the rest of my life, any more painfully. And it was only 10:30 a.m. The small, hardwood stage was mere steps away but may as well have been as distant as a million miles. I looked up at the thick timber trusses supporting the roof of the R.G. Lee Chapel on the campus of Florida Baptist Theological College and wondered whether my prayers would go any higher. Why bother?

Instead, I seethed.

Little more than a week earlier, God had called me into ministry. At least I thought He had. But for what—to humiliate me?

God, I jumped out of the boat. What else do You want?

*Lord, this giant has called out my name all my life, and now
You're letting him laugh at me?*

I leaned forward and rested my elbows on my knees, the wooden pew creaking beneath the weight of my burdens. It was 1990 and I was 20 years old and in utter turmoil—mad, confused, and feeling a new brand of dejection. But those emotions weren't alone. A familiar voice echoed through the bare rafters, off the high walls, and into the chambers of my heart. Inexplicably, the voice was almost comfortable, almost welcome. I thought I had left him back home in Alabama, but he travels well. You can't miss his whisper in an empty chapel.

I sighed. It was the same old, same old....

Fear.

M

I have these buttons in the back of my head. Even after 15 years as a youth pastor and more than two years as a recording artist, they're still there. They're the reason I almost bailed on becoming a youth pastor or even thinking about writing a song. They're the reason I've always lived scared.

From the time I was a small boy and even into adulthood, my first instinct always has been to shrink away from challenges. I would see an obstacle ahead of me, and, just when I almost convinced myself to face it, Satan would press the perfect little button at the perfect little time. When it involved ministry, it was worse. Anytime I was sure God wanted me to attempt something, the enemy jumped on those buttons with both feet:

*Boy, there are a million reasons why you're not good enough to do that. Should
I start naming them?...*

We all have our buttons, don't we?

A few of mine are a little different. One is dyslexia, which essentially means I don't read well. I can't give you its scientific explanation, but, in layman terms, there is a hiccup somewhere between the page and my brain telling me what the page says, and I lose my spot. You wouldn't believe how big a disadvantage this precious little gift presents.

That's only one of my two biggest buttons. As a kid I also was tested for ADD—Attention Deficit Disorder—and I passed, thank you very much. It was the only test on which I ever scored a perfect 100. I started yelling, "Yeaaahhh!" My mother was wailing, "Nooooo!"

I understood that dyslexics could not read. That was simple to grasp, even for a child. But I just couldn't absorb the ADD talk. They tried explaining it, but I really wasn't listening. I just knew that they abbreviated it for us so we could get on to something else. Otherwise, I'd be going, "Yeah, I've got Attention Defic...Hey, what's that shiny thing over there?"

I was tested for ADD just prior to third grade. I could still pick up on most things because I wasn't totally dense, yet my funniest memory of that day is how long it took them to explain ADD to me. Remember, the lady had administered a test that revealed to her that *I'm not listening.*

All through the hour-long, follow-up discussion, I was thinking, *"Why are we still talking?"* I had already counted the ceiling tiles. "Brady Bunch" episodes ran through my head.

It's wonderful that God has brought me to a place where I can joke about it now, but it wasn't always so. In fact, I was 21 years old before I ever spoke the word "dyslexia" aloud. How's that for a button? Satan made sure I always saw myself as tiny. Anytime I considered doing something bigger than myself, he reached out with an unmanicured nail and punched a convenient button....

You step out, boy, and I'll show them who you really are....

You know what I've learned? Once Satan tells you that you have a problem, he then tells you that you're the only one with that problem.

My childhood church didn't really help me handle my shortcomings. I guess we were just tremendously blessed, but somehow my family attended the perfect church. Sure, a lot of people were sick, but nobody sinned at my church. At prayer meetings, people always mentioned lungs, brains, hearts, kidneys, and feet with gout, but there were no marriages in trouble, no one had unforgiveness in their hearts, no one lusted or coveted, and no one was bitter. I had ADD and dyslexia, so it didn't take me long to come to one unmistakable, unspeakable conclusion: *I'm messed up.* So one of my earliest lessons from the body of Christ was to keep my mouth shut.

At the same time, I watched my church and had another thought: *"You guys are messed up, too."* No safe haven here. No refuge.

There went a chance for help.

Next, Satan stripped God's Word right out of my hands. He punched the dyslexia button, and I quickly learned not to take my Bible to church so I wouldn't have to read aloud. Did you have the same Sunday School teacher I had? The one who used the small, square, pea-green room with rainbows on the walls and cutout Bible characters on the blue felt board? The one who sat you down in tiny wooden chairs to read verses for an hour because she didn't study her lesson?

By the way, now that I'm a youth pastor, I understand her dilemma. I realize now that she must have been thinking, *"I've got 45 minutes with you little beasts. Turn to Leviticus."*

When my parents made sure I carried my Bible or the teacher had one available for me, I switched tactics. I learned to count ahead. When we sat in a circle and took turns reading, I'd determine the sequence and prepare to read my verse; if there were five kids ahead of me, I'd go down to the sixth verse and start rehearsing. I'd read and read, memorizing as best I could. Then, invariably, it would happen. Some kid ahead of me would go to the bathroom and throw off my count. It meant I would have to try to read a different verse than the one I had memorized! One day it struck me: *"Hey, that kid who went to the bathroom is probably dyslexic. He's just smarter than I am."*

My fear led me to avoid anything written, which I now regret. I wish I had discovered 2 Corinthians 12 long ago. It would have revolutionized my middle school years. That's where Paul tells the story of having buttons in the back of his head, too. Take a moment to digest what Satan didn't want me to read:

> So to keep me from being too elated by the surpassing greatness of the revelations, a thorn was given me in the flesh, a messenger of Satan to harass me, to keep me from being too elated. Three times I pleaded with the Lord about this, that it should leave me. But he said to me, "My grace is sufficient for you, for my power is made perfect in weakness." Therefore I will boast all the more gladly of my weaknesses, so that the power of Christ may rest upon me. For the sake of Christ, then, I am content with weaknesses, insults, hardships, persecutions, and calamities. For when I am weak, then I am strong.
>
> 2 Corinthians 12:7-10

Paul took time off from starting churches and writing the New Testament to pray for himself. Imagine that. All he could think was, *"God, if I were just younger,"* or, *"If I could have a degree like him,"* or, *"If I could just sing like her,"* or, *"If I were just taller, thinner, faster, or bigger…"* He had all these reasons why God could use him if he were just somebody else. And that was me. When I finally discovered that Scripture, it could not have hit me with more punch had it been written in flashing neon. I always had assumed God could use other people more powerfully than me.

It was an amazing breakthrough: The one exercise Satan most tried to prevent in my life—reading—was the very one that most empowered me. His scare tactics had worked for so long…too long. It was time for my weakness to make me strong.

I dived into God's Word. Slowly, I built discipline into my prayer and devotional life. I began asking God what He was saying to me through particular verses or passages. I began praying Scripture back to Him, which, incidentally, leaves you certain never to pray outside of God's will. I was saved at the age of nine but was well into my teens before I discovered just how personal a God that Jesus is. It seemed as if my buttons started shrinking.

Then one day it came.

At 20 years old I sensed God's call to ministry. Today we would label it a paradigm shift. Back then, it just felt like an earthquake. For years I had spent great energy inventing ways to stay off of anything that resembled a stage, especially if it meant being up there alone. I believed ministry took place only upon the stage, and most of the time it involved wearing a tie. This "call of God" thing, then, was a tad disconcerting.

Satan began tap dancing on the buttons. I was pleasantly surprised at my response. For perhaps the first time, I discovered that greater is He who is in me than he who is in the world. (1 John 4:4) For the sake of the story, I strain to remember exactly what went through my head the day I jumped into the great unknown, but I can't recall. I do know I just jumped.

In one week's time, I moved out of my parents' home in Montgomery, Alabama, married Melanie, moved to Graceville, Florida, and enrolled in Florida Baptist Theological College (now named The Baptist College of Florida). Because I sometimes sang with my dad in church, I thought, *"Well, maybe that's where I'll go into ministry—music."* I had no clue what else to do because most of my interests lay in drawing and painting, and I couldn't see making a living in that field.

So there…I had my major. Music, it was.

Try to picture this: I'm coming off of the greatest whirlwind week of my life. God's hand seems heavy upon me. I'm tiptoeing through the tulips of a honeymoon. I'm unpacking boxes in a sparsely appointed new campus apartment. I'm registered for classes. I'm totally absorbed, touring the campus in orientation class. And I finally remember something.

I don't read music.

I don't read *words* well.

But music?

Half notes? Whole notes? Fortes? Treble clefs? Crescendos?

Never heard of them…couldn't spell most of them.

It was a long day.

They herded all forty of the music majors into a large suite, and I quickly learned that these musicians were the best of the best from churches all around. You sing? Big deal. Everybody sings here. You play an instrument? Whoopee. The janitor plays a meaner guitar than you ever could.

Stay in a small enough bowl and you can be a big fish. Suddenly, I was Nemo in a vast ocean, and Dr. Patrick Malone, the head of the music department, walked in and brought with him my old friend, Fear. The professor just smelled smart, you know? How could I have known he would become one of my greatest, dearest mentors? When I first saw him, I remembered that, to me, sheet music resembled Egyptian hieroglyphics. I was almost trembling. He began explaining the day's itinerary and then opened the doors to the bomb bay. The words almost echoed:

"We're going to take a test today."

Please understand, the word "test" does to me what blue lights in your rear-view mirror do to you. I don't do tests. Even if I know an answer, I can't figure out how you're asking the question to share with you what I do know. Some of you know what I mean.

Doctor Malone continued, and by now I could scarcely hear him through the bass rhythm of my pulse in my ears: "We're going to take a test today, guys, and you're going to have two hours to complete it. We're going to decide from the results of this test where you're going to begin in your major—or whether you should even major in music at this college."

I sat in dazed silence, staring at the floor as he passed out the test. Doctor Malone prayed, and when he said, "Amen," it was like the sound of thunder as students grabbed their pencils in unison and began shredding through the exam. I was in the back of the room, watching their pages turn, one after another. It looked as if they were writing in a coloring book. It was nothing for them.

I swallowed hard and worked up the nerve to start reading the test, only to confirm my fears. I didn't know any of the answers. Not one. I kicked into survival mode and wondered, *How am I going to get out of here without anyone noticing?*

Eight minutes into the allotted two hours, I signed my name on this test with no answers and walked past these people. I could feel them looking up at me. I reached the front of the room, placed my test facedown in front of Dr. Malone, and quickly and quietly slipped through the door. I was already consoling myself with the notion that at least none of them would ever see me again—because I was going home, back to Alabama. It was almost poetic that I had placed my blank test atop a giant piano before leaving.

I began walking across campus toward our apartment, mulling over what I was going to say to my new bride and to my family. I was all alone, no one else around. I'm not sure, but I think I heard a muffled snicker....

Boy, you gonna soar with the wings of eagles, huh?...

It was a straight shot from the music building to our apartment. Yet God, in His sovereignty, had thought a hundred years before that day to plant this large chapel between my apartment and me. The sidewalk led straight inside, and I was drawn, as if compelled, through the front doors. It was empty. I sat down in the back, wounded and bewildered—just wounded and bewildered enough to reflect over the past week and to decide that God wasn't playing fair. Why was I in Florida and not in Alabama if this weren't of God? Why was I at a Bible college and not at art school if the Lord hadn't directed me? All those years of trepidation and yet I had ignored the buttons and broken through, and when I finally did something for God, wasn't the sun supposed to shine? When I finally was obedient and took the big step, weren't the birds supposed to sing and the baby angels would descend and play their harps for me? People would prayerfully decide to give me cars and houses because I was obedient, right?

I don't know how long I sat there. A while.

I was just working up a good spiritual lather when the faculty began prepping for chapel service as dozens of students streamed in from behind me. The seats quickly filled, and I had never been in one room with that many people, some 500 students and staff. I stared straight ahead and tried to keep to myself. Several students went onstage and stepped up to the microphones, and I recognized some of them because I had just accompanied them through freshman orientation.

They started singing, and they were awesome. The kid on the piano? He was unbelievable. All I could do was sit in the back of that chapel and mutter under my breath, "Now, see God, those are the kinds of people you need. Do you see how good they are? People would listen to them for hours."

I didn't register a word they sang or a word preached. Everyone filed out after the service, but I stayed in the back. After a while, someone turned out the lights, and I heard the slam of a solitary door.

It was 10:30 a.m., and I stewed as I stared at the grand piano through the stained-glass hue. I didn't know it then, but it was another of those Sovereign God moments. I eased out of my seat and walked toward the piano, which was so big that they couldn't lift it, so it sat at the foot of the stage. Otherwise, I never would have approached it. I wasn't going on that stage.

I sat at the piano and began playing around with the only four chords I knew. In past years, I would sit at my church piano after everyone left and play my chords, and they sounded so cool, you know? They didn't sound cool anymore. Satan reminded me of what I had just heard out of that very piano only moments earlier:

Boy, this doesn't sound anything like that guy who was playing a while ago. He was awesome...

That's when my stewing finally boiled over. There, at the grand piano in an empty R.G. Lee Chapel on the campus of Florida Theological Bible College, I had my first fight with God.

My indignation was a lava flow: "God, what's the deal? You know how I get. You know I get fired up sometimes, but I always seem to catch myself before I do something really dumb. But I'm in Florida. I've stepped out. I've left home, I've left the state, I've gotten married, I've dragged my wife down here, and she's working her first day on the job at this very moment to pay for this. My church gives me this big sendoff service and they all come by to shake my hand because *Mark's going to go do something great for God.* My parents are probably still on the phone, calling all the relatives to talk about how proud they are. And here I am, about to come home on Day One because I am not good enough for this."

Oh well. You can't read sheet music through tears anyway, can you?

God started teaching me a lesson that day, one that He's still teaching me. I know it's the reason I became a youth pastor and songwriter, and I'm sure it's the reason Casting Crowns exists. That morning, at my lowest, He drowned out Satan's lies and in His still small voice whispered, "Mark, I don't need you. I want you. …Mark, I don't need you. I *want* you. …Do you think all of your fears and limitations and everything that makes you feel so small are worrying Me?…Do you think that all of the initials with which you were diagnosed by those childhood tests are weighing Me down? Mark, I am going to do something in the world. I just want to know…do you want to come?"

I *so* wanted to come along.

I went back to school the next day. And the next day, and the next day, and the next day. And six years later, I graduated from this four-year college. Hey, those initials may not weigh down God, but they sure made my bookbag heavier. Algebra was my favorite class. I took it three times. The teacher and I were really close after a while.

I learned to lean on the Lord's help, and He was faithful, of course. I realized life as I had lived it would not work in college because I could no longer coast. I had to bear down. I had to concentrate. I had to deal with my buttons.

The Lord placed me in an English class with a dyslexic professor, Bruce White, and before long he began recognizing a few traits in me.

"Are you dyslexic?" he asked.

"No."

"Shut up. Yes you are."

"OK."

Our relationship grew, and he encouraged me to write because he noticed that I had a knack for drawing pictures with words—if someone made me.

God is still making me draw pictures with words. Now I'm a youth pastor for about 400 teenagers at Eagle's Landing First Baptist Church just outside of Atlanta, and I still have no idea what I'm doing. I sit in my office sometimes and mutter, "Well, this is it. We're going down today. There is some committee meeting somewhere in the church right now and any minute they're going to walk into my office and say, 'Brother, (you know it's bad when they call you "brother"), we've been talking, and we're really not sure what you're doing, and we don't think you know either.'"

On those days—and I have them often—God has to remind me:

Mark, if I'd wanted someone else, I would have called someone else....
You get up there, dyslexic boy. You show the world what I'll do through somebody who will let Me.

I have spent 15 years saying things I'm not sharp enough to say. I write songs I'm not good enough to write. I'm constantly part of circumstances that are so far above me that they frighten me. I'm swimming in the deep end because God doesn't need me. He *wants* me. He told me so at that great, big piano in that great, big chapel.

For it was at that very moment, on a day shaded in all the subtleties of blue, that the Lord gave me the song about those waves and giants in my life. You now know it as *Voice of Truth,* but it wasn't called that at first. No, for years I called it by its original title.

Fear.

My trembling fingers played it for the first time in the only four chords I knew.

Introduction

GODLINES

The temptation was almost too much to bear.

Moments earlier, several little tykes had scrambled into the dentist's backyard, eager to be the first to try the slide. Or the swings. Or the highest tower. For most of the kids, it was a rare privilege to enjoy a play set so monstrous that I dubbed it "Six Flags." I was youth pastor at Center Hill Baptist Church in Loganville, Georgia and did not have kids of my own. But when I joined other church members for fellowship at the dentist's home, I learned something about people just from watching the kids.

It was in the fall, and the 6 p.m. shadows were growing longer by the minute. Behind the play set from Mars was a fence with a small gate. And beyond the fence were woods so thick that, especially at that hour, they appeared almost black. I sat inside and grinned as I watched the children's reaction to the play set.

Then something curious happened. I've never forgotten the lesson.

After about five minutes of racing around and through the wooden play set—with all of its towers and gadgets—the kids gravitated somewhere else. The next time I looked out the window, every kid was lined along the fence, near the locked gate, all straining to look over the top of the fence. All that was beyond the fence were the woods—the black, mysterious, unsearchable woods. Behind the kids was Six Flags, the most entertaining play set they could ever imagine. It was theirs to enjoy. But in front of them was something they couldn't get to, something they couldn't have, and it mesmerized them.

Aren't we all just like those kids? God provides us so much and charges us with His specific tasks for each of us, and we happily dabble for a while. But when those five minutes grow old, we start looking elsewhere.

But that looks awesome over there...

Well, why does that catch your eye?

I don't know...I just wish I could go over there...

God used those kids to teach me an object lesson that has helped me remain focused on His exact purposes for my life. Like most people, I have needed occasional reminders that God has a plan and purpose for every life He creates—some of those purposes are universal and apply to all of us; some are specific to the individual. All are designed for the glory of God.

So it is with my songwriting.

I'm a youth pastor at heart. That is why I am here on this earth. God gave me not only talents and gifts but also the *desire* to minister to students. He called me to this ministry by ambush during my first year in college. When I came to this fork, I took the road less traveled, and it has made all the difference.

It also has been a tremendous challenge, and not only because of the perils inherent in shepherding young people amid our oppressive culture. It also has been a challenge to me on a personal level—to my hopes and dreams, my philosophies and beliefs. Sometimes I've been able to stay the course and remain focused on God's charge. At others, I've jumped off the play set and wandered over to the fence.

One area I have strived to stay within God's direction is music. Obviously, it is an enormous passion. As with most passions, it can easily misdirect my focus. I intentionally did not chase a career in music because I knew my calling was in student ministry. I always have used music as a tool to reach and teach students, and if the Lord wanted to make it something more, well, that was His prerogative.

I'm humbled that He chose to exercise His prerogative in such magnanimous fashion. This book isn't big enough to adequately express how I feel about His grace and graciousness. I don't always understand God's ways. I can't always clearly see where He's taking me. I just know that Psalm 75:7 makes it clear that He is unquestionably sovereign:

> *But it is God who judges;*
> *He brings one down, he exalts another. (NIV)*

I still wonder exactly why He has chosen to exalt our band, Casting Crowns. We signed a record deal with Beach Street Records under Reunion Records more than two years ago. Most of the band members worked as leaders within our youth ministry at Eagle's Landing First Baptist Church in McDonough, Georgia before we were "discovered." While marriage and ministry have prompted a few moves, the band members remain leaders within the youth ministries at Eagle's Landing or other churches. I continue to serve as co-youth pastor at Eagle's Landing along with Reagan Farris, one of my former students.

I have led student ministries at five churches in Georgia, Alabama, and Florida. At every stop, the Lord has grown our ministry and grown us, and music has been one of His common threads. I brag only on Jesus when I report this: At last count, 35 of my former students now serve in student ministries or as worship leaders.

Perhaps now you better understand why my lyrics are so direct and often are aimed at the Church. Because of my heart for youth ministry, my songs often include themes impacting the body of Christ. Therefore, I'm not thinking about the world's potential reaction when I write a song. Usually, I'm just writing it for the youth group and the families in our church. While my audience has grown a little over the past few years, I still try to write with a pastor's heart. Most often, I write songs with particular people or situations in mind. I have learned that God doesn't fit into any kind of box—CD or otherwise. He has astounded me by using these songs to connect with so many other people and other kinds of situations, and we hear from those folks on a daily basis.

A prime example of God's providential use of our songs is *Praise You in This Storm*. I wrote the song after befriending Laurie Edwards, a mother in Thomasville, North Carolina whose 10-year-old daughter, Erin, was suffering from bone cancer. Little did I know that the *Lifesong* CD that included the song would be released one day after Hurricane Katrina decimated New Orleans and the Gulf Coast. The words to that song took on a whole new meaning to thousands of hurting people throughout the country. The lyrics hauntingly fit.

I didn't do that. Only God could orchestrate such incredible timing and applicability, which is why I've come up with a term for how He gives me lyrics: *Godlines*.

It is a weird moment when you realize *this song exists now*. Beforehand, there was nothing. Now, there exists this body of work that even feels alive. Jesus is the Creator God (Colossians 1:15-18), and His creativity cannot be measured, but it is breathtaking to catch a glimpse of Him at work.

That's the way I feel when I'm writing songs. I have learned that God already has said everything there is to say. It's all in His Word. But when it comes to songs, I believe they all belong to Him and He knows how He wants them written. For some inexplicable reason He has chosen me to hear certain songs first. My ministry is to share them with everyone else. I literally have sung a lyric aloud or played few notes on the piano and thought, *"Man, He chose me to hear that!"* The definition of a Godline, then, is to write a lyric or paint a picture or write a sentence in a book or speak a point in a sermon or share a loving word at just the right moment and realize: "That was not me. There is no way I came up with that."

I can tell you where the Godlines are in every one of my songs, so I decided to close the chapters of this book by sharing each Godline with you.

Often, I get a chill when the Lord gives me a Godline, and when I first write a song I usually cannot sing it for a good month because I cry through it. I know I didn't come up with the song, so it feels like a gift. God let me hear it first, and that touches me.

Not to say that I don't get in the way. When I write a song, I become glued to it until I finish, and usually I think it's the coolest song ever written. Ever. It's going to change the world and everyone will become missionaries. But then I give it a day or two and let the new song buzz wear off. That's when I sing it again and say, "OK, that's terrible." So I start over. I work and I wait. God always shows up.

Sometimes, I have worked on songs for months or even years. Sometimes, they come together in a matter of days. I compose and write them in my head and never commit them to paper or computer. In the last few years, I've taken to singing into a microcassette recorder because I was forgetting too many lyrics and melodies. I realize that my approach is dangerous, and many times I've tripped over old lyrics still bouncing around in my head or forgotten songs altogether. I lost the song *In Me,* which appears on *Lifesong,* for six months somewhere within the recesses of my brain. I was probably 24 years old when I began working on the song and had most of the lyrics completed. Then the song slipped away. About six months later, I was in the car with my dad when he said, "Hey, whatever happened to that song where you sing, 'When I'm weak, He makes me strong; when I'm blind, He shines His light on me'"? I cocked my eyebrow and looked at him.

"Oh yeah."

So I finished the song.

I retain most of the songs because I'm so passionate about them, and it has been a tremendous blessing to learn that others have become passionate about them as well. The response has been indescribable.

Someone recently asked me, "What is it about your songs?" My answer, other than the fact that I get to hear so many Godlines first, is that I honestly don't know. To me, we're not saying anything that hasn't been said countless times by many other people. Nothing is new. I try to paint pictures of people and scenes because I think storytelling helps songs, but there are a number of good storytellers in Christian music.

I'm a product of Christian music. I grew up listening to Steven Curtis Chapman sing songs like, "Heaven in the Real World," and asking hard questions like, "Where's the hope? Where's the peace?" I remember a 4Him song that said, in effect, "We're living in a real world with real hurt and real pain, and all we really need is the real thing." I've been ministered to for 14 years by DC Talk, who were never scared to say anything that needed to be said. I've always respected that about them, because they were so popular and easily could have crossed over to mainstream music and done their own thing. But their songs unapologetically go straight back to the Gospel. The Newsboys are the same way. Toby Mac, Third Day, Delirious, Michael W. Smith, and Chris Rice are other wonderful ministers.

Some of my favorite songwriters are Jon Foreman of Switchfoot, Martin Smith of Delirious, Nicole Nordeman, Chris Rice, and Cindy Morgan. There is such a gut-level realness to what they say that it's like you're listening in on their conversations instead of hearing a song. It doesn't seem like it would ever be performed onstage. Rather, it's like they're sitting in your living room and sharing with you, because it's right there where you are.

My point is that we aren't alone in this ministry of Christian music. However, I have been humbled by the reaction to our songs, a reaction that perhaps comes because we try to say transparently what God wants us to say. We try not to shoot from above but from below, because we know we rub shoulders with everyone else in this life's great struggle. We don't mind saying,

"Here's how we messed up, but here's how God is working." We're broken people just like everyone else. Maybe that's why folks seem to identify with us.

I can't help but let the youth pastor in me give a closing thought.

I'm convinced that any uniqueness Casting Crowns enjoys is because I've listened to Christian music exclusively since I was 22 years old. I'm 36 now. It wasn't a decision of whether certain music is right or wrong, good or bad. To me, it was a decision of what's wise of me to plant in my heart. I realize what I listen to comes out of me—and I believe that is true of most people.

If I were to listen to some of the old, secular music I once enjoyed, it would be like my saying, "I don't live my old life; I'm just a fan of it." Jesus starts getting into my head a little bit in Matthew 5-6 and asserts, "All these things concern your heart. These are heart issues." What does that say about the music I absorb? For me, listening to secular music is like saying, "This isn't who I am, but I wouldn't mind being it for a day—or at least reminiscing." That just doesn't compute.

Still, I don't stand on a soapbox and preach not to listen to certain music. I do tell students that what we listen to matters, and it's a question of wisdom. Ask yourself, "What's wise for me?" Andy Stanley preached a sermon at AtlantaFest one year that changed a lot of my perspective, and I remember his words: "What's the wise thing to do? In light of who I am, who I want to see myself being, and what my future goals are, what is the wise thing to do?"

Therefore, what I listen to does matter. What I watch does matter. Everything matters. We are spiritual beings, and everything that touches our lives has spiritual implications. (Philippians 4:8)

I'm committed to availing myself completely to the Lord. It is the only way I know to hear from Him, and I would rather hear His take on life than that of someone from Nashville or Los Angeles. I know of no other way to write songs. The best ones always come when I wait on Him.

Did you notice the Bible verse at the beginning of this introduction? It is Psalm 40:3:

He put a new song in my mouth, a song of praise to our God. Many will see and fear, and put their trust in the LORD.

God honors His Word. I saw Him do it night after night in the fall of 2005. In the first half of the Lifesong tour—on which we partnered with area churches and were joined by evangelist Tony Nolan—more than 14,000 people asked Jesus into their hearts as their Savior. Psalm 40:3 came alive: He put a new song into our mouths, just as He said. Many saw and put their trust in the Lord, just as He said.

My lone goal in writing is that people will connect with God through this moment, this story, this verse, this chorus, this topic. The topic is not even the goal. God does not need a song to communicate His truth, but I hope that each song grabs people's attention and reminds them, *Hey, this is what God has to say about this subject.* Songs, then, become tiny little devotions that point us to the Lord, remind us of Him and His Word, and maybe shake us a little bit. I want us to think about our individual relationships with the Lord in some area. When we are glorifying God with the talents and gifts He has given us, we are fulfilling at the highest level our purpose and God's plan.

Every song—as does every person—should have a point and a purpose. The Colossians passage I mentioned earlier states: *All things were created by Him and for Him.* They were created *by* Him and *for* Him.

Godlines included.

What if His People Prayed?

If my people who are called by my name
humble themselves, and pray and seek my face and
turn from their wicked ways, then I will hear from
heaven and will forgive their sin and heal their land.

2 CHRONICLES 7:14

DUST ON THE SWORD

I had seen her many times in many different settings. I had seen her on television news and had heard about her on the radio. I had read her story in magazines and newspapers. And I had seen her countless times at church. Occasionally, I even knew her name.

Sometimes she had blonde hair, sometimes red or brunette. Sometimes she looked like she had the world neatly wrapped up in a bow; at other times, I could see only the weight of her baggage. Sometimes I spoke to her, sometimes I watched others glance at her and whisper. Always, somehow I knew she was hurting.

Who is this girl? You know her too. She works beside you. She's in the car next to yours during rush hour. She's in front of you in the checkout line at Wal-Mart. She's in your daughter's class at school. She's in your church's youth group.

Or maybe she's your child.

Maybe she's…you.

As a youth pastor, I have seen this girl more times than I can count. She's the girl—whatever her name, pedigree, or appearance—who tried to fill her life's voids with empty choices. She shows up a lot in my life. In fact, she shows up on both of our albums.

The girl who became the subject of the song *Does Anybody Hear Her?* on the *Lifesong* CD actually spawned a different song first. *What If His People Prayed?* emerged after I caught a brief glimpse of the girl on the run.

I was watching television news footage of a picket line of church people screaming at this little teenage girl. She was running through a gauntlet of angry people and holding a newspaper over her head as she tried to enter an abortion clinic. I did not see love. I saw condemnation. I saw a frail statistic weaving her way through the catcalls. All those behind-the-back whispers had turned into full-frontal screams.

I muttered, half-audibly: "Those were the last 50 believers that girl passed by on the way into that clinic to kill her baby, and that's what they had to say to her: "YOU'RE A MURDERER FOR KILLING YOUR KID!" I thought, *"You know, we're putting all of the weight on this girl to live right when she's not equipped to live right."*

Yes, the girl was making a terrible choice, an abomination in God's sight. Yes, she was willfully taking a human life formed by God. (Psalm 139:13-16) But, no, I don't believe our venom is the answer.

The whole scene left me with some questions. If the Church had been living for Jesus in front of her beforehand, would she have been in such a predicament? How many ingrown churches did she drive by when she was deciding whom to date? How many silent Christians did she sit beside in the lunch room when she was deciding where to go in this relationship with this guy? How many of us were around her at one time or another and didn't have any opinion or anything to say about her life until she did something on our bad list, and then it was time for us to say what we think? Is this not an upside-down way of thinking?

Second Chronicles 7:14 came to mind. Bill Clinton was in the White

House, the courts were upholding abortion rights and getting friendlier with gay rights, and Christians were united primarily by grumbling and sitting on their hands. It seemed as though everything I heard was, "What's wrong with the world? It's the government's fault that this is happening. The schools are doing this, and the politicians are doing that." The government, the schools, and the media were always the problem. They're easy targets, and we've proven it by pounding on them.

I'm all for speaking truth, but we seem to forget one obvious truth: They're lost. Lost people sin. That's what they do. There is no compass in them telling them anything else to do. We, however, have a compass that points to true north. So 2 Chronicles 7:14 casts a different light on these issues.

I read it and think, *"Maybe it's us."*

Maybe it isn't the rest of the world all the time. Maybe the big, bad wolf isn't the big, bad wolf after all. Maybe if we would follow just one verse, I wouldn't see this girl so often:

If my people...who are called by my name...will humble themselves, and pray ...and seek my face...and turn from their wicked ways...then will I hear from heaven...and will forgive their sin...and heal their land.

Look at God's promises. He will hear our prayers. He will forgive our sins. He will heal our infirm nation. He reveals all of these promised blessings, and yet we're constantly praying that God will cause those very changes. We're saying, "God, heal the land. Feed the poor. Bring revival to our country. Why aren't You moving, Lord? Why is all this stuff happening?" And we've forgotten the first half of what He says. It's an if/then statement. It's conditional. He says, "If MY people..." God is calling His people to follow Him, strip off all of the façades and lay aside all of the sin, including our "pet" ones, and start loving Him with our lives.

Do you want revival in the land? Do you desire a nation after God's own heart? Then make sure your heart is the first in line. Ask Him for revival, but ask Him to start with you.

It's really not the world's fault. The world is the world, although it will be held accountable in the end. Every knee will bow and every tongue will confess that Jesus is Lord. (Philippians 2:9-11) But the Church's accountability supersedes that of the world: "For it is time for judgment to begin at the household of God; and if it begins with us, what will be the outcome for those who do not obey the gospel of God?" (1 Peter 4:17).

Ironically, the growth of this song reflected my personal growth. It first was titled, *What If the Whole World Prayed?*, but that changed during the recording process. It was a hard decision to alter the title and chorus of an entire song because, frankly, the original sounded better. The words *What if the whole world prayed?* just sang better. But it wasn't scriptural. A conversation with Steven Curtis Chapman, who was helping us in production, convinced me that it had to go.

"You know, if you really think about it, the world's praying is not really what you're talking about," Steven said. "The world isn't saved. They can't pray."

And that is true. The only prayer God will hear from someone who doesn't know Him is, "Please save me." (Proverbs 15:8, 29) We all were enemies of God until He redeemed us. He's not going to hear anything else a lost person prays, because an unbeliever actually is an enemy of God. (Romans 5:10; Colossians 1:21; James 4:4)

It wasn't the first time this song had undergone radical change.

Initially, it was a soft piano song, but you wouldn't know it by its anthem-like rock chords now. The first verse was essentially what you hear today. The original second verse demonstrated how heavily the familiar young girl was on my mind:

What if the church put down their signs,
Crossed the picket lines,

Dried a young girls tears,
And shared with her the love of Christ?
Before another unborn baby dies,
When will we realize?

I changed the music from a piano ballad because I thought the desperate message was being lost in the music. I changed the second verse because I thought it merited its own song. It needed more attention; it was greater than just an afterthought. What began as that second verse is now *Does Anybody Hear Her?* on our second CD, and it took me nine years to write that song.

I replaced the second verse with one that re-emphasizes the first, most important function of the Church, which is prayer. The verse's questions are simple: What if WE, the army of the Lord, picked up and dusted off our swords? What if we prayed for the government and lifted up the politicians? Wouldn't that prove a greater solution than our consorting about how bad they are?

I make that assertion fully aware that this song sounds like I'm pointing fingers. It's amazing, but even though this song was never released to radio, it includes a line that has prompted more questions than almost any other single line I've ever written.

What if the family turned to Jesus,
Stopped asking Oprah what to do?

People are fascinated with that line. At concerts, we pause the music to let the audience sing it, and the crowds greet no other line with as much gusto.

Here's the kicker: I've never gotten the first e-mail or criticism about that line, which confirms for me that I communicated my intentions. Some people wondered whether it would prove controversial, but it was never about talk-show host Oprah Winfrey. It was about us, the Church. It was about our exalting people and taking advice from others instead of finding counsel in

God's Word. (Psalm 118:8) I never intended to portray Oprah as an enemy. Rather, she's just another voice out there.

Right about the time the album was coming out, someone approached me. "Do you think Oprah will ever hear this?" he asked.

At first, I thought, *"Who's going to ever hear this record?"* I honestly doubted that it would reach very many hands. But as the album started doing well, more people began asking, "Have you gotten any calls or anything?"

I dismissed them: "Oprah ain't studying me. She's got a much bigger world to live in than I do."

I never worried about whether I had offended Oprah or anybody else, because even in the back of my head I knew I was not trying to be condemning.

It wasn't about grandstanding.

It wasn't about pointing fingers.

It was about pointing us to Jesus.

It was about our getting answers from the Lord and not from people… whether we're talking about the most powerful woman in the world. Or a little frightened one ducking the picket line with a newspaper over her head.

THE GODLINE

I was alone in the huge sanctuary of First Baptist Church of Daytona Beach when I hit the song's chords as they appear on the album, changing it from a piano ballad. I knew it worked right away because the first verse fit the music perfectly:

> *What if the church, for heaven's sake,*
> *Finally stepped up to the plate,*
> *Took a stand upon God's promise,*
> *And stormed hell's rusty gates?*

The Lord gave me this verse by reminding me of Matthew 16:18: "And I tell you, you are Peter, and on this rock I will build my church, and the gates of hell shall not prevail against it." After reading that verse, it dawned on me that gates are not offensive. They're defensive. So let's charge the gates. In the song, I saw hell's gates as rusty. That was key, because I wanted to draw the picture that the enemy is losing the battle. He's losing people every day and will lose even more to a body of Christ that is on mission—and on mission in the right spirit.

THE BOTTOM LINE

- Read Matthew 7:2-4. How often do you struggle with judgmental thoughts, and what do you think is the source of these thoughts?
- Can you think of an occasion when you or someone you know took a proper stand on an issue but did it in the wrong spirit? What was the outcome? How could the situation have been handled better?
- In what areas do you think the Church is failing its New Testament mission? In what areas is the Church strong?

If We Are the Body

My brothers, show no partiality as you hold the faith
in our Lord Jesus Christ, the Lord of glory. For if a man
wearing a gold ring and fine clothing comes into your
assembly, and a poor man in shabby clothing also
comes in, and if you pay attention to the one who
wears the fine clothing and say, "You sit here in a good
place," while you say to the poor man, "You stand over
there," or, "Sit down at my feet," have you not then
made distinctions among yourselves and become
judges with evil thoughts?

JAMES 2:1-4

FROM DAYTONA TO VENEZUELA

There is a low roar over the city for two weeks every summer. Bike Week in Daytona Beach, Florida is known around the world as Motorcycle Mecca for bikers of every stripe. Every single one of them, it seems, trusts in the biker mantra "Loud Pipes Save Lives," because their exhaust pipes harmonize in a guttural roar that can rattle windows. Into this strange world, I hesitantly strode with the Gospel.

I was a fairly naïve kid growing up in southern Alabama. I was raised by godly parents in a conservative small town and experienced very little of the world as a teenager and young adult. Needless to say, Bike Week left an impression on me in my years as youth pastor at Daytona First Baptist.

As I reflect upon the development of Casting Crowns' first radio single, *If We Are the Body*, I recall my most educational Bike Week experience.

I was helping a small band that attempted to perform as an outreach during the middle of Bike Week. It was really whitebread music, and I remember thinking, *"Man, we're going to get killed."* We didn't quite fit the culture of the area, and we turned a few heads when we shuffled onto the scene, set up our equipment, and began playing.

I was only a bystander, but I noticed that it was as if we had an anti-cultural force field around us, and no one came inside this giant circle of about 500 yards. Everyone kept their distance—everyone except one road veteran. Nearby was a little old lady who was drunk. She stood back all alone, swaying to the music and waving her arms in the air while yelling in her raspy Southern drawl, "I love the Lawwwd! I love the Lawwwd!" At least somebody there claimed to know the Lord.

Otherwise, we weren't exactly welcomed by a city of restless vagabonds. In the middle of one of our songs, I grew self-conscious. I began noticing what I was wearing. It was the strangest feeling of being caught in a time warp: I was 32 years old and feeling peer pressure again. It dawned on me that everyone around me had the shirts, boots, denim, and leather inherent to the motorcycle culture. I was standing there in Duckhead shorts and sandals. If I was going to be all things to all people so that I might by all means save some (1 Corinthians 9:22), I figured I'd better find something in black really fast.

Juan DeVevo, one of our guitar players, was with me. I grabbed him and explained I was getting nervous. "Let's go find a shirt or something to kind of fit in." When I address students now, I certainly can't say peer pressure is not real. I was reminded very quickly during Bike Week, when I almost feared for my safety.

Juan and I waded into rows of tents set up by merchandisers. There are thousands of bikes everywhere and hundreds of tents where these Bikers would shop.

We looked for a T-shirt shop with a decent selection so we could find something other than "Death to the World," or, "Kill 'Em All, Let God Sort 'Em Out." We finally found something vanilla and headed to the checkout line.

While in line, I became fixated on an interesting scenario unfolding before me. I noticed that I wasn't the only one with Duckhead shorts and sandals. There were several people dressed just like me, and they were in line with their new biker gear—just like me. We were going into the tent as Regular Joes and walking out as "bikers." It was a surreal moment as I studied these folks. I felt like I had a great reason to try to fit in—attempting to share the love of Jesus—but I wondered about the motives of some of these other guys. I wasn't alone, either.

As we neared the cash register, I noticed a man at the entrance of the tent. He was probably 60 years old. His face looked like it was made out of some of the leather he was selling. I can only presume it was his tent. He apparently made his living by traveling from one road show to the next, and he was sitting in his favorite rusty folding chair. It was filthy and looked as if it was held together only by the hundreds of stickers accumulated from his travels. Seated directly in front of the girl working the cash register, the guy was wearing all black and a bandana on his head. Much of what he had earned in selling t-shirts he had then invested in various tattoos. His beard clung to the top of his cheeks and flailed over his chin to hide his neck. You smelled him before you saw him. When you think "biker," you envision this guy.

As I watched him, I noticed that he was watching us. He spent his time staring at people go through the line and fork out money to buy his wares. What I remember most was the look on his face. All those people in line were his bread and butter, but he was disgusted by them. It was obvious. He was watching all these people file past with their bags bulging with new biker gear, and I could almost see him thinking, *"So you're a biker now?"* His contempt was apparent, yet business wisdom won out. He had decided he'd sell black T-shirts and leather vests to wannabes for the rest of his life.

I thought nothing more of that moment until about two years later. I had already moved from Daytona to Eagle's Landing when, out of the blue, I thought of the old biker and his tent.

We were hosting the leadership of a visiting missions organization with whom our youth group was partnering for a trip to Venezuela. The missions leaders brought with them a teenage girl from that country. I learned later that she was so poor that they had to buy her some presentable clothes just to join them on the trip.

She was wearing those new clothes when she walked into the gym where the missions leaders would address our youth during our Wednesday night worship service called *Refuge*.

None of our students welcomed her. No one struck up a conversation with the obvious stranger who looked a little different. All of our youth began flowing in around her, and she just sat there, listening to all of their conversations. I tried to imagine everything our Venezuelan visitor heard from all these girls swarming in around her while not really paying any attention to her. I looked at the girls to her left who probably were talking about what someone else was wearing, while the girls behind her were sharing what they did the weekend before or what they were going to do the following weekend. Surely, the visiting girl must've heard it all.

Then she sat back and watched all these same girls stand when the music played and raise their hands in worship.

Our kids still didn't know the identity of this visitor or why she was there. No one had talked to her. Billy Edmunds, the leader of the missions group, took the stage to educate everyone on Venezuela. Then he introduced the Venezuelan teenager, who emerged from the heart of the crowd and joined Billy onstage.

The first thing the Venezuelan girl did was pray. In Spanish. I sat back and wondered what the girls who had sat around her were thinking: *"Wow, she was just sitting here among us and we didn't notice. She's just like us...."*

When the Venezuelan girl finished praying in Spanish, she looked up and began speaking in English. You could hear people breathing. Those girls around her had to have thought, *"She heard everything we said."* As I listened to her give a heartfelt appeal to come to Venezuela, I couldn't help but wonder whether she was thinking in the back of her mind, *"You are going to come to visit us? No way. This place isn't real. I don't know who you people think you are."*

I don't know. Maybe the Venezuelan teenager never had such thoughts. But if she made any effort to listen to the America that was around her that day, I believe she could not have helped but noticed the superficiality. That's when I remembered the leathery old biker in his tent, peering at the contemptible masses as they filed past.

I'm thankful that our youth ministry has matured since that day, and we have many core kids who are solid believers.

Still, there are a lot of kids—and a lot of adults, not only in our church but in every church in the country—who are wading in the kiddie pool of faith. If I may use the term, they're wannabes. They're Bike Week believers. They're everywhere. They're buying the T-shirts and the fish logos and bumper stickers and they're learning the lingo and they're learning to never say "yes" or "no" to anything—only to promise to "pray about it." They always have to "feel a peace" about things.

Do you know why I know them so well? Because I used to be in the same spiritual checkout line.

We in the Church practice all of this learned behavior. But for me there was an inner disgust to sit in a sanctuary and know I wasn't the believer I professed to be. When we constantly struggle with such thoughts—the inward feeling that something is askew—it shuts down a church and leaves it dead.

I realize my views may seem strong to you, but they have been formed over years of watching us grab our stuff and fall in line with everyone else. It has been a source of friction in my spirit for years, which explains *If We Are the Body*.

This was the first Casting Crowns song released to radio. And for that I'm thankful, because more than any other song it gave us an instant identity. It is bold. It is direct. It is simple yet unapologetically makes the point that the Church is not living up to God's expectations as outlined in 1 Corinthians 12-13 and James 2. In fact, the song was a little too direct for some Christian stations who thought it too "preachy" and refused to play it.

One of the reasons I felt comfortable in writing such an outspoken song was because I once was a surface Christian. Now that I'm learning a life of faith, I look at my students and I see myself two decades ago. I look at the Church and realize how far short of God's blessings it is treading. I couldn't help but try to grab the lapels of its finely starched jacket and say, "Hey, you're missing so much...."

It was about 1993. I was not only a newlywed but also a youth pastor in Samson, Alabama while attending college and working as a janitor at a bank in Graceville, Florida. Between the round-trip school commute and the nights all alone cleaning toilets in the bank, I had plenty of time to hum a few bars, and that's how *If We Are the Body* was born.

I was really growing in my walk with the Lord at the time. As I thought about how to reach the kids in my youth group, I reflected upon my years of attending youth group as a teenager. I realized how ingrown we were and how we viewed ministry as something performed only by the men wearing ties onstage. They preached, and we all sat in the pews while they did ministry for us. Our job was to stay quiet, which we didn't do very well.

I don't know where I missed it. Please don't interpret this to mean that no one in my small church ever said, "You need to go out and love on people." Still, somehow that message was never drilled into our students. Before I knew it, I was a young adult in charge of a youth ministry, and I started seeing in my students the very kid I had been as a teenager. I thought, *"Whoa, we are waaaay off here."* Church was like a club for us. It was a place for us to come and get away from everything else. It was more a refuge for the body of Christ than it was for the world. Instead of it being a place for the world to find hope, it was where we secluded ourselves to find hope.

I made a decision. I was *not* going to walk into this youth group as their new pastor and promptly teach them to become evangelists. That may catch you by surprise. Allow me to explain: One of our shortcomings in the Church is how we treat new believers. Instead of weaning them from milk and helping them grow deeper in the Word and service, we yank them into a class and tell them to get out there and reach people.

Yet those new believers haven't even forgiven themselves for their pasts. They still loathe themselves. They may be a sweet-smelling aroma to the Lord, but Satan makes sure they still smell their own stench. In fact, there are people who have been in the Church for years who still aren't ready to spread the Gospel. We're not close enough to God to see what anybody else would want with Him, so it becomes only a duty that we are to fulfill The Great Commission. The last thing it is at that point is a labor of true love—for the Lord or for a lost world.

Again, the reason I'm so strong on this point is because I've been there myself. I grew up with *The Four Spiritual Laws*. I was supposed to find people and read this to them, but I wasn't personally walking with Jesus. I was not living the truth I was trained to share.

So I dived into Scripture on my own, and the Lord lifted so many layers of scales from my eyes.

First Corinthians 12 peeled away a big layer. I learned that everybody has a ministry in the Church. Ministry isn't reserved for only the people onstage. I once thought that if you didn't sing or act or speak—or if you weren't off in Africa wearing one of those little missionary shirts—you weren't in ministry. I mistakenly believed that I was just part of the audience. Eventually, I discovered that there is no audience in the Body of Christ. There are only believers. *We're* the body. We're the hands, the feet, the ears, and the toes, and when everyone in the body isn't performing ministry, the body suffers. It limps and crawls. It doesn't work. I was trying to show my kids that we're the first and primary way that Jesus is going to love on others. He's got to love them through us. That's His design for the Church. We are their clearest picture of Jesus, and how we act is how they're going to see God.

If We Are the Body actually was first titled *This Should Be the Place*. I began working on it in my infancy as a songwriter, and it included this chorus:

This should be the place
Where everyone fits in.
This should be the place
Where anyone can find a friend.

Like I mentioned, I was just starting out. Stop laughing.

Hearts are searching for love
To call their own.
In all the world,
This should be the place.

I try to paint vivid scenes in every song I write, and it's readily apparent that *If We Are the Body* was written by a youth pastor. I simply tried to relay stories and scenes that I was seeing. In my mind's eye, I still can see the situations described in the verses. I can see the rough-looking traveler straggle into the worship center and slip into the back pew, looking straight ahead while everyone glances at him and no one smiles. He has come seeking *our* refuge, remember?

I also can see a girl walking into our youth group at the time and our kids didn't even know she was there. Even those girls in the seats directly around her were concerned only about themselves. The visitor didn't fit in, so they didn't want anything to do with her. They were just being teenagers, but the difference between being a regular teenager and a teenager who is a believer is that somebody who has God in them wants Him to leak out on other people.

Whether they come from across the street or from Venezuela.

I'm sad to say that, too often, the girl in this song shows up on Sunday mornings and isn't welcomed in any language.

It's crowded in worship today,
As she slips in, trying to fade into the faces.
The girls' teasing laughter is carrying farther than they know,
Farther than they know…

THE GODLINE

Quiet nights working as a janitor at a bank in Graceville gave me the perfect opportunity to work on this song. I had a small salary at the church and Melanie and I were barely making ends meet. We were eating crackers and peanut butter, so I needed the extra job. It turns out that I needed it for more than one reason. It was a great time of personal worship and reflection.

I remember having much of the song completed but still feeling I had missed my original mark. I was trying to hear something different with it, so I changed the music for the verse. While singing it differently, I rediscovered what it was saying. That's when the song changed.

I'll never forget the day I sat there and thought, *"If we are the body, if we're His hands and feet, then why aren't His hands and feet doing what they're supposed to do?"* Suddenly, out it came. I remember the first time I sang that line aloud: "If we are the body, why aren't His arms reaching?" I got a chill. I was alone in this room, and I knew the Lord had given me something. I had never heard the 1 Corinthians message phrased that way. I certainly had never thought of it in those terms before.

It seems so simple now, reading the words on paper. But isn't that how God works? Simple truth, like the Gospel, impacts hearts most. Always has, always will.

But if we are the body,
Why aren't His arms reaching?
Why aren't His hands healing?

Why aren't His words teaching?
And if we are the body,
Why aren't His feet going?
Why is His love not showing them there is a way?
There is a way.

THE BOTTOM LINE

- Can you think of an occasion when you failed in an opportunity to reach out with the love of Christ and kept to yourself?
- Why do you think you failed to act? What will be different come your next opportunity?
- You are an integral part of the body of Christ. Where and how are you using your God-given gifts? If you are not consistently serving Him, what is the reason?

CASTINGCROWNS.TV

VIDEO CLIP - "If We Are The Body" from the *Live From Atlanta* DVD
You've read it! Now go watch & listen to these stories at
www.castingcrowns.tv

Voice of Truth

For God has not given us a spirit of fear,
but of power and of love and of a sound mind.
2 TIMOTHY 1:7 (NKJV)

ONE VOICE

I didn't have a clue as to what I was doing. I could tell you only that I was a freshman in college, newly married, and that Jesus had called me to His work, which apparently meant saying "yes" to the fellow who walked up and asked me if I'd like to be a youth pastor while pursuing my degree.

My first response was, "You've got to be kidding."

Me? Work with teenagers? Which one do I strangle first?

But there I was, standing in this small, country church called New Zion Baptist outside of Bonifay, Florida. It was near my college in Graceville, which was convenient for tooling back and forth as a full-time student and part-time pastor. I had eight kids in my ministry. I had never been responsible for one kid, much less eight. I remember thinking, *"All I know is I love Jesus and I almost like these students."*

Five weeks later, everything changed. It dawned on me one day that, even if I wasn't making an impact on these kids, they certainly were making one on me. I told Melanie, "Oh, my gosh. These are awesome people. These teenagers are just incredible."

Suddenly, I thought about them all the time. I related with them unlike anyone I had ever related with before. I wanted to be around them constantly, and I invented ways to ensure I would: We ate together, we hung out, we played volleyball in the back—anything to assemble with my new best friends.

Word got out in those north Florida backwoods, and before long I was staring at 30 faces on Sunday mornings. My intent was to make them as passionate about Jesus as I was—I knew I wasn't the Holy Spirit and couldn't *make* them do anything, but I was willing to die trying.

I took them to a youth conference in Montgomery, Alabama, my hometown. There must have been 6,000 teenagers in attendance, the most people I'd ever seen in one place. A traveling youth speaker named Dave Edwards was the keynote. It was 1991. That I remember Dave's name 15 years later should signal how profound an experience I had.

In the middle of his testimony, Dave Edwards paused and said, "Oh, yeah, I'm dyslexic."

I snapped to attention. I looked up and caught myself thinking aloud, "What did he just say?" Dave began telling one dyslexic joke after another as I stood wide-eyed and frozen. The whole room was roaring in laughter, but I was so amazed I could only think: *"What are you doing? You've lost your mind. Who in the world is going to want to hear what you have to say now?"*

To me, the subject was off-limits. I had pictured my own dyslexia and ADD as such debilitating weaknesses—I had so suffered their existence and feared their consequences—that it took everything I could muster daily to bury them. I had conjured up the picture that no one possibly could respect someone who does not read well. Even first-graders can read!

I don't remember Dave's jokes. I was too astounded that he had even broached the subject, but he gripped me terribly. I wouldn't completely realize it until God worked on me for several more months, but because of Dave's testimony I could never be the same youth pastor. I had witnessed a level of authenticity that would render me a counterfeit if I tried to ignore the lesson. It took a while for these seeds to truly blossom in my ministry, but they were sufficiently planted. I just needed to do a little more weeding.

My hoe would be a little song called *Fear.*

For the song's history, flip back to my testimony at the beginning of this book. It was my response to the overwhelming anxiety of launching out in a life surrendered to Christ when all I had ever known was the embarrassment of dyslexia and ADD.

After hearing Dave Edwards, *Fear* became my song of testimony. Slowly, I warmed to the realization that, to let the Lord have his way with the song, I would have to let Him have His way with me. Eventually, *Fear* became my staple, my lifesong. I couldn't sing the song without telling the story, because the song is my story.

For years, *Fear* was just a full piano song—a piano, the lyrics, and never anything more. No strings. No guitar. No drums. The song nevertheless always garnered more reaction than any other song I had written. Even today, every time I sit at a keyboard and tell this story—whether it's in a small church or an arena—it's brand new because there are so many new people God is using the song and the story to reach.

The song traveled with me through my various ministry stops and was always a favorite. I kept it a sparse piano ballad even after I joined Casting Crowns in Daytona Beach and we migrated as a youth ministry and band to Eagle's Landing. *Fear* appeared on our first independent CD, which we recorded in Daytona.

Ironically, it was not on our second independent CD, recorded after we moved to Atlanta. That CD was entitled *What If the Whole World Prayed?* (the precursor to *What If His People Prayed?*), which through a mutual friend fell into the hands of Mark Miller, lead singer for the acclaimed band Sawyer Brown.

Mark Miller has other friends. Some of them own record labels. It's not what you know, it's Who you know. We both know Jesus, and the Lord miraculously brought about The Record Deal That Just Doesn't Happen.

One of Mark Miller's friends is Steven Curtis Chapman. They partnered to form Beach Street Records under Reunion Records, which is a division of Provident Label Group. Provident is owned by Sony-BMG, one of the world's media giants, and, somehow, these people were listening to our songs to decide which ones to put on our first commercial CD. My head was swimming.

Steven is the reason the song *Fear* is now called *Voice of Truth.*

Mark and Steven had selected the songs they liked from our second independent CD, but they had never heard the first independent CD we recorded while we were in Daytona. So they had never heard *Fear.* Even on the CD, it was just a piano song; the melody and the verses were exactly the same as the current version. The original was slightly different, however.

It had no chorus.

Both versions include the waves and the giants calling out my name and laughing at me. But the difference in the original song came when I sang, "Boy, you'll never win, you'll never win." I went on to sing the line a third time before immediately returning to the introductory chords. No chorus. The song didn't resolve.

The closest I came to a resolution, Scripturally and spiritually, was through a third verse at the song's end. That verse is now the bridge, but with subtle differences at the end:

The stone was just the right size to put the giant on the ground,
And the waves, they don't seem so high
From on top of them looking down;
I will soar with the wings of eagles,
If I could just ignore the sound
Of the waves and the giants in my life.

Finally, I concluded the song with a gentle prayer:

Lord, You've not given me a spirit of fear,
But of power and of love and a sound mind.
So from now on, I won't let the tempter's lies

Turn my eyes away from the prize
That You have set before me.

I played it for Steven. He listened intently and smiled.

"Man, we need to do something with that," he said. "I've got this idea that might be neat to go with that. You're mentioning all these voices that are talking to you in your life. But what does the voice of truth say to that?"

One thought led to another, and the *Voice of Truth* trumped *Fear* right there in the room.

Keep in mind that just a few weeks before this moment, the only world I knew was student ministry. Student ministries love Christian music, and there is no bigger name in Christian music than Steven Curtis Chapman. I would have been content to sing the rest of my life in an iron-beamed gymnasium on a stage we had to set up and tear down every single Sunday and Wednesday, yet there I was writing a chorus with the artist whose songs I had sung in church for years.

Steven and I entered a tiny recording room, so small that our knees were almost touching when we sat down. It was about the size of a closet. I was still trying to absorb the notion that anybody outside of our church was interested in our music, and now there was only a recording microphone between Steven and me. He was wearing a baseball cap, shorts, an untucked shirt, and loafers.

"Here's what I'm thinking," Steven said. "I want to play it on my guitar, and you sing what you've been singing."

Steven began plunking away on his guitar, his head bobbing with almost every stroke. I was supposed to sing on cue, and all I could think was, *"This is STEVEN CURTIS CHAPMAN right here with ME!"* I could hardly remember the words to the song, much less sing them. I quickly told myself, *"Don't blow this. Don't blow this."*

I drew a deep breath and started singing. When I listen to those old tracks now, I can tell that I'm singing a little weird because I was trying to grab the gravity of this little hero moment. It was only nervousness, however. There wasn't enough room in that closet for the waves and giants.

In a moment, I reached the lines about the waves calling out my name and laughing at me and then closed with the customary, "You'll never win, you'll never win...."

But I didn't sing "You'll never win" a third time. Steven cut in with his new chorus.

But the voice of truth tells me a different story,
The voice of truth says, "Do not be afraid."
And the voice of truth says, "This is for My glory."
Out of all the voices calling out to me,
I will choose to listen and believe the Voice of Truth.

I thought, *"Hey, that's good."* When he sang the chorus a second time, I joined him, dabbling with different harmonies. We also worked together to hone the last few lines of the chorus. Two singers with one heart. One voice.

That was it. My lifesong *Fear* had turned into the *Voice of Truth,* which is such an irony, such a God-Thing, considering my history and the song's context.

You see, what started as my personal prayer of anguish at a piano in my college chapel crystallized one day in a tiny recording studio that opened onto the grandest of stages. In between, there were countless nights of sharing my testimony and my incomplete version of the song, and there were instances of incredible growth and spiritual enlightenment that God used to prepare me for both the tiny studio and the grand stage.

One of those occasions came at the aforementioned youth conference in which the Lord emboldened me through the genuine transparency of speaker Dave Edwards. It was on that night—the first time I'd ever heard anyone have the audacity to stand before a crowd and admit he suffered dyslexia—that a young singer walked onstage to lead worship. I had been singing his songs for a while, but it was the first time I ever saw him in live concert.

His name was Steven Curtis Chapman.

THE GODLINE

The channel that introduces the chorus of *Voice of Truth* talks first about waves and then giants taunting me. That channel is the song's Godline.

But the waves are calling out my name and they laugh at me,
Reminding me of all the times I've tried before and failed.
The waves, they keep on telling me, time and time again,
"Boy, you'll never win, you'll never win…."

When I composed and sang those lines, I realized it was the first time I completely captured what I had been enduring my entire life. I knew many Bible stories about people accomplishing great things, but in my mind I forever would be inadequate. I thought maybe one day I could be the guy who knew the guy who climbed out of the boat and walked on the water with Jesus, but it could never be me. Or maybe I eventually would be in the same church with the guy who killed the giant—or maybe I could see him on tour one day as he came through my town. I would never get to be the conqueror, though, because of the following shortcomings…and I would mentally list them as Satan reminded me of each hangup.

I guess those were the waves and the giants talking, right? Peter fell into the water only when he started listening to the wrong voices. He heard a crack of the wave, and it distracted him from Jesus. He got a little spray in his face, it drew away his attention, and he started listening to the wrong voices.

I've done that throughout my ministry, and the Lord has used this song and this particular Godline to minister to me at every turn. One transforming moment stands out.

My first ministry after college was as youth pastor at Center Hill Baptist Church. God moved mightily, and a youth group of about 15 or 20 reluctant kids multiplied to become a ministry that basically ran itself. They formed their own ministries. The teenagers were leading worship; the leaders were teaching small groups; the adult volunteers were overseeing the whole ministry, and the group was abounding. In mid-stream, I discovered how easily the wrong voice could still sidetrack me. And I thought I was so mature....

One day a letter arrived. It was from one of my students. He had decided that I was the worst youth pastor who had ever sucked in a breath because I apparently did not spend as much time with him as I did with others. It was a long letter with a crisp message: "I don't even know why you're a youth pastor."

Guess what? I bought it. I read his letter and sat there and thought, *"He's right. I'm a terrible youth pastor. I play favorites."*

For a good three days, I listened to Satan speaking through a person. I was so distraught that I didn't know what to do. I wondered, *"Should I call him in and beg his forgiveness? Should I pull in the leaders and poll their opinions on my leadership? Should I address the entire ministry and apologize?"*

Stumped, I began sifting through my desk drawers, searching for something, when I stumbled onto a box full of Polaroid photos.

"What in the world is this?" I muttered while opening the box. Most churches keep photos of their new members or baptisms. This box was packed with snapshots of teenagers who had come into the church since I had been there. I had forgotten about the box.

I flipped through the pictures and saw kids who months ago had visited the church for the first time and sat in the back, not wanting to be there or to be bothered. Most of them had been dragged to church by parents. And now some of those students were small group leaders. I saw a girl who would've been scorned by most Christians because of her past. I had a picture of her with her entire family and extended family that had become fully involved in church. At first, she had come alone. Now her entire family was with her.

I looked at the next picture and remembered another life God had changed through our ministry. I looked at the next picture, and the next picture, and the next picture, and I recognized the fruit of persisting and loving on people. I saw the wisdom of our approach to ministry. It wasn't about Mark

Hall having some great student ministry. It was about letting people reach people—giving away the ministry to God and to others and seeing what He does through them.

In that moment, God reminded me of my Godline. I was listening to the wrong voices—the waves and the giants. I wasn't listening to the truth. I was letting Satan use people to hurl stones at me, and God reminded me to operate on truth, which is His voice, and His voice alone. I still have that long-winded letter somewhere. It reminds me of the day I made up my mind:

I will choose to listen and believe the Voice of Truth.

THE BOTTOM LINE

- Name a time when you have listened to the wrong voice. Think through that entire scenario. What was the result?
- Do you have weaknesses that the enemy consistently attacks? How do you help him? How do you guard against him? Have you searched God's Word for ammunition to wield in response?
- What is your greatest fear? Why? Can you identify areas in your life or ministry in which this fear has diminished your effectiveness or even paralyzed you? Have you searched out and memorized God's promises in answer to your fears?

CASTINGCROWNS.TV

VIDEO CLIP - "Voice Of Truth" from the *Live From Atlanta* DVD
You've read it! Now go watch & listen to these stories at
www.castingcrowns.tv

Who Am I?

For he knows our frame; he remembers that we are dust.
As for man, his days are like grass; he flourishes
like a flower of the field; for the wind passes over it,
and it is gone, and its place knows it no more.
But the steadfast love of the LORD is from everlasting
to everlasting on those who fear him...
PSALM 103:14-17

HEADED HOME

I t was dark, and she was behind the wheel of her car, headed home.
Jessica Wolfe, a beautiful young lady with big brown eyes, shoulder-length
blonde hair, and a perfect smile, had celebrated her 20th birthday two days
earlier. Her boyfriend, 23-year-old Scott Devlin, was following Jessica in his car
as they returned from Scott's former college campus to Jessica's hometown of
Kouts, Indiana. Jessica had surprised Scott that morning by showing up at the
screening of a video he had edited for his alma mater, Grace College in
Winona Lake. She had worked third shift all night and had driven the 70
miles to see the video's debut in chapel service.

But she didn't mind. That was just Jess. She loved people, which is why she
cherished her job at a home for mentally handicapped senior citizens, and she
loved Scott. Both had accepted Christ in their childhood and were strong believers. Though they had dated for only two-and-a-half months after Jessica's sister
introduced them, Scott was intending to marry her. Scott and Jessica spent a fun

day with friends at the college before climbing into their vehicles for the short trip back to Kouts.

Scott introduced himself to me through e-mail. I'll let him tell the rest of their story.

E-mail: Thursday, October 14, 2004; 8:33 PM

Mark,

I am writing in hopes that this note along with my little story will reach you and the rest of the band. My name is Scott Devlin and I am 23 years old, residing in Warsaw, Indiana. I recently had a special young lady in my life by the name of Jessica. Jessica was an absolute example of what it means to be in pursuit of Christ. It is because of this trait that Jessica and I were heading down the road toward marriage. You see, Jessica also loved your album, especially *Your Love Is Extravagant*. She would play it over and over for me, singing the words every time with such passion. A little over a month ago, I was following Jess to her house on a dark stretch of road in the midst of a thunderstorm. It was only 60 feet in front of me that Jess lost control of her car and rolled top-first into a tree.

As I made my way to the car and reached inside the twisted metal, I knew instantly that Jess was already with her Lord. I spent the next 10 minutes covered in mud, in the middle of a pouring rainstorm, complete with crashing thunder and flashing lightning, holding on to the hand of a lifeless and empty body that once contained the soul of a 20-year-old girl I loved.

Your Love Is Extravagant was played for 500 people at Jess's funeral, where at least three people came to know Christ the way we do.

I still cannot listen to the song without tears welling in my eyes—not because of a loss, but because I remember the passion with which she sang those words. Your song *Who Am I* has been the reality of this experience for me. God is still God, and He is in control of His world. He gives and He takes away.

I have seen evidence of both.

The purpose of this e-mail is not to tell you a story about a car accident —something that happens many times a day. I am writing this e-mail to say thanks. Thank you for sharing your heart through your music, especially through *Who Am I* and your rendition of *Your Love Is Extravagant*. Jess could sing your songs and see God through them. … Please continue to share what you have special in your life with those who need to hear it. What you do makes a difference.

Press on and God bless,
Scott Devlin

Scott works as a counselor at Lifeline Youth and Family Services, but on the side he pursues another passion. He is a drummer in a Christian band named The Avenue. The group has a unique ministry, performing only large outdoor concerts and attempting to grab the attention of passersby who come upon these large worship gatherings.

The Avenue played two nights after Jessica's death. Her family was in the front row. Everyone knew Jessica's story, and everyone knew her family was there.

"They had their hands raised high and their eyes closed, and they were praising God with everything they could give. Two days after Jess died, her family was giving God glory and praise," Scott said. "The people at the show were saying, 'Look at that: Her family is in the front row praising God. Her boyfriend is on the stage praising God as he plays the drums.' And they said, 'I want that.' There were people who broke down and accepted Christ because they saw us worshipping that night. They could not grasp how that was possible.

"People would come up to me afterward and say, 'I'm so sorry,' and I said,

'I'm not, because I wouldn't trade one of these salvations to have Jess back.' I don't want her back. She wouldn't want to be back. I would give her up over and over again if it meant people finding Christ. To me, that's the most important part. To me, that's why it happened. That's why I can keep going and praising and worshipping God, because I know that He is still using Jess to bring people to Him."

M

It was dark, and I was behind the wheel of my car, headed home.

As Thanksgiving 2000 was coming to a close, I was in the middle of nowhere—physically and spiritually. In the blackness of a nighttime road trip, I suddenly became consumed with one question: Who am I?

Who am I…to be chosen of Him?
Who am I…to deserve God's grace?
Who am I…especially in light of who He is?

The setting and the questions provided a perfect backdrop for a few simple lyrics to bubble unexpectedly to the surface. How could I know that the words the Lord sparked in me as I traveled over the rolling hills of north Alabama would have such an impact more than four years later? It also would surprise me that a song born behind my steering wheel that night would almost be an afterthought on the first album—in fact, it would not even be completed until after our first radio single, If *We Are the Body*, was climbing up the charts.

It was late, and I was driving my family home to Daytona Beach after visiting relatives. Highway noise can be the gentlest of lullabies, and Melanie, John Michael, and Reagan had drifted off shortly after we began our eight-hour return trip.

Maybe it was the spirit of the Thanksgiving season. Maybe it was the glances at my rear-view mirror to see my little ones snoozing in the backseat.

Maybe the trip along backcountry roads, my little family plugging away in the vastness of it all, had me thinking. I cannot tell you how unnerving it can be for a guy with ADD and a sleeping map-reader to drive narrow roads in the black of night. I know there is a God, or else we all might have been singing *Where Am I?*

I know there is a God for many reasons, though, and at that hour I couldn't help but worship Him. In this conversation with Jesus, it hit me.

You know, who am I to think that I can just pray anytime that I want to—like I can just pick up a phone and call God and He's always going to be there? That's awfully presumptuous. How arrogant it is to take that for granted, as if God is just waiting on me to call anytime.

The truth is that He is waiting for me to call anytime. He is available, but it's not because I deserve it. I suddenly realized that it's a terribly big gift to assume—the gift that I have such a relationship with the one true God that He purposely hears me, that He even knows me at all, much less knows *my name* and my cares.

I thought of the trite nature of so many of my prayers. While this cursed world seemingly spins out of control and disasters of varying form and degree crush humanity on every continent, sometimes I care enough only to pray for my headache to go away. Or for Melanie and the kids to have a good day at home. Or for quick passage through Atlanta traffic so I can make a meeting.

That's where my mind was that night, thinking of our giant world and all of its real problems. I was left thinking, *"Well, I just need to shut up because God is so big and there are all of these atrocities and starving people...."*

Amid all of the questioning, my Christianese kicked in.

In my best regal, baritone voice, I triumphed as I thought to myself: *"Well, I'll tell you who I am...I'm a son of God, I'm a child of the King, I'm a royal priesthood, I'm a holy nation, I'm a chosen people, I'm more than a conqueror, I'm a new creation...."*

And all of that is true. With all of my heart I believe those fundamentals. But truth wasn't under question; motivation was. Since I believed I held all of those positions, it was almost as if I thought I deserved that God would hear me.

At the end of those questions, I had moved past the Christian jargon and trying to convince myself that I deserved Him or His favor. Instead, I slowly migrated to a deeper understanding: *Mark, really, you're a vapor. You're no bigger than a minute. You're here and gone. Nobody is going to remember you in 100 years, because you're not the point here. So the truth that you're so small and so broken and so self-destructive and so self-absorbed yet God cares about you anyway? That's what you should share.*

I decided to share that message through music.

In reflecting upon the song's development, I've realized its big truth is that, before you can truly understand who you are in Christ, you first must understand who you're not. I believe that is where I had missed it. I had mistakenly viewed my relationship with God from one of two wrong perspectives:

- **Entitlement:** This occurs when an imperfect, broken person believes he or she deserves something, anything, from a holy God. It surfaces in puffed-up pronouncements like, "I'm a royal priesthood. I'm going to go out and kick some butt." We get to that point by thinking that we're something we're really not because of something that *we* have done: "I *came* to the Lord. I *found* Jesus." The Bible says that no one seeks God. No one. (Psalm 53:2-3)

- **In the red:** Pastor John Piper describes what he calls "The Debtor's Ethic."[1] It is a works-based approach in which everything a believer does is out of duty to repay Jesus. No one can repay Him. It's impossible—so this approach to a relationship with God is impossible.

This song tries to land right in the middle. I hope it helps hone our understanding of our relationship with Him.

It reminds us that God says, "I'm huge and you're not, but I love you anyway. This is all because of Me, not because of you. You didn't do this. It's not because of who you are. It's not because of what you've done. It's not because you decided one day, 'I think I'm going to be noble today and come to God,' because there was nothing in you that sought Me. Yes, you are more than a conqueror now, but not because you did the conquering or already were something worthy."

At that thought, the song really started coming together in the glow of the dashboard lights.

It all began with questions like, "Who am I that God would know me?" but then it took a lot of twists and turns. I wrestled with some weighty notions. I tinkered with different melodies. I changed certain words and tried to fill in the blanks. There was a point where I almost got sidetracked and God had to bring me back. He spoke to my heart and said, "The question isn't just *who you are,* but look at *who I AM.* In light of how big I am and how small you are, My love for you looks even bigger. You're really starting to grasp a tiny sample of how big My love is. It's huge. Remember, I have a lot of distance to cover to get to you."

That's how God gave me *Who Am I?*

Can you believe that it was a rock song at first, a power ballad? Most of the current lyrics were plugged into a bold anthem. Over the following months, I was glued to this song. I couldn't stop working on it, tinkering with it in my head. Rarely do I commit anything to paper or computer, and this was no exception. Fortunately, I did not lose any of this song, probably because I couldn't let it go, but it morphed on me. The words were getting lost in a wall of sound, so I pared it down to more of a piano song.

Fittingly, I was behind the wheel of my car again in Daytona Beach when I finally nailed down the first verse. I still remember singing for the first time....

Who am I?
That the Lord of all the earth,
Would care to know my name,
Would care to feel my hurt?

When I listened to it, I said to myself, "This could either be a really cool song or it could be a really cool message." Remember, I'm a youth pastor, and

I'm forever thinking in terms of either songs or sermons. The song is not the point. The song is a tool. If it ever becomes anything more than that, no one will ever remember it.

I'm thankful I remembered it, because I had tucked away *Who Am I* in my congested mental file and eventually moved on to other songs. Four years later, after ministering at Eagle's Landing First Baptist for a few years and then landing our record deal, I blew the dust off of it.

I was in Mark Miller's studio trying to finish our debut album. The song *If We Are the Body* was already an advance release and being received well by the public. We were trying to figure out exactly which songs would complete the CD.

I sat down at the piano and in my choppy playing tried to sample this old song that had started on the Thanksgiving trip home from Alabama. I couldn't even play all the chords—the building crescendo in the middle of the song is hard for me to pull off—but even with my plunking it out on the spot, Mark looked at me, raised his eyebrows, and said, "That's a good song."

Until that point, it had never really registered with me that it could be something special. But isn't that the way God works? He uses the foolish to confound the wise and the simplest of ideas and hearts to produce great harvests. I've written songs about which I thought, *"Hey, that's a pretty good message. That turned out neat."* But initially I wasn't overwhelmed with *Who Am I?* Finally, I said to myself, "Well, I'll just share it with them and see what they think." I had a personal attachment to the song, but I never imagined it would make the record. And I certainly never fathomed it would generate such amazing feedback.

Remember how writing this song helped deepen my understanding of my standing before God? Music charts don't mean much to Him. He's interested in much grander emphases. The way He has used this song has left me, at times, without a good response—just dumbfounded. I'm sincerely humbled by the myriad of stories that have poured in, all sharing how the Lord touched some part of people's lives through this song.

Among the most moving was Scott Devlin's e-mail about the death of his girlfriend, Jessica Wolfe. He said later that God used *Who Am I?* to help him heal, to help him realize God is still on His throne and yet only a whisper away.

"That was a song following her death that just seemed to come out of everywhere. It was always playing somewhere. It was always on the radio," Scott said. "I remember sitting at my desk and reading the lyrics one night and breaking down and saying, 'Wow, this is incredible.' Despite all I've been through, the tears I've shed, the horror I've seen, this song reminds me that it's God who is in control. I am nothing and He is everything. And He loves me enough to show me that there is life beyond death. I have more to live for. Yes, this was tragic. I don't wish this on anybody. But I have more to live for, and I'll get to see her again some day.

"So I have no fear. I have no reason to worry about where she is. I live life with no fear because I don't fear where I'm going after this life. I stand on the truth of God's Word and know that He is in complete control and this happened for His reasons. That song, it glued it all together."

I read such testimonies as I sit in my little office in McDonough, Georgia, and I'm left muttering yet another question: "How did we get to be a part of that?"

Who am I, indeed?

THE GODLINE

I should share two Godlines for this song because I'm capable of generating neither of them. The first Godline was the wonderful little channel that the Lord gave me that leads into the chorus.

Not because of who I am,
But because of what You've done.
Not because of what I've done,
But because of who You are.

It all started in my head as a building crescendo of words and melody. When I write songs, I have to think of the words and music at the same time. They almost always occur together in my head. The first line came to me: "Not because of who I am, but because of what You've done," but the music was incomplete. When the music came to me, the channel simply finished itself as "Not because of what I've done" naturally followed. Sometimes the words and music birth each other, and that's what happened here.

The second Godline for this song is one I shared earlier in this chapter. It's the very first verse, and I vividly remember sitting in my car and singing it aloud for the first time:

Who am I?
That the Lord of all the earth,
Would care to know my name,
Would care to feel my hurt?

As soon as I sang it, I smiled and thought to myself, *"Yeah. That's good stuff."* That's one of those moments where you say aloud, "Thanks, God. That was cool."

THE BOTTOM LINE

- What is your view of God's sovereignty? Could you provide a Biblical perspective of God's sovereignty if someone asked you?
- What has been your perspective of your relationship with Christ? Is it Scriptural, or is it closer to "entitlement" or to the "Debtor's Ethic," and why?
- Do you know the believer's position in Christ? What Scriptures do you use to support your belief?

American Dream

"Everyone then who hears these words of mine and
does them will be like a wise man who built his house on
the rock. And the rain fell, and the floods came, and
the winds blew and beat on that house, but it did not
fall, because it had been founded on the rock.
And everyone who hears these words of mine and does
not do them will be like a foolish man who built his
house on the sand. And the rain fell, and the floods
came, and the winds blew and beat against that house,
and it fell, and great was the fall of it."
MATTHEW 7:24-27

HE WORKS ALL DAY

I was stuck in traffic, mind wandering, when I noticed the bumper sticker. On a BMW.

It attracted my attention for two reasons. First, I'm not accustomed to seeing bumper stickers on luxury vehicles unless it's one of those European capital block letters that apparently mean something on highways overseas but I'm still not sure exactly what; and, second, the phrase on the sticker raised my eyebrows. The yuppie in the Beamer was proudly announcing, "Whoever Dies with the Most Toys Wins!"

With a mixture of indignation, pity, and knowing concern, I watched him drive away, no doubt letting his nose sniff out the next grindstone to pay for his toy with the gaudy bumper sticker.

"He doesn't really believe that, does he?" I asked myself, and tucked away the moment in my mental file. A youth pastor never knows when he'll need a good illustration....

M

Casting Crowns was playing at Carowinds amusement park in North Carolina, and our office manager, Susan, was manning our merchandising table when the lady approached. She picked out a book of sheet music for our songs, and, while paying for it, asked a favor of Susan.

"Would you please express to the band how much their music means to my boys?" the lady asked. "Their father has left, and *American Dream* is what we're living."

Touched by the lady's predicament, Susan grabbed an autographed photo of the band and slipped it between the pages of the song book before handing it to the lady. "I put a little something in there for you," Susan said. The lady smiled, thanked Susan, and disappeared into the crowd.

A few minutes later, the lady returned, this time with tears streaming down her cheeks.

She has *two* boys, each a huge fan of Casting Crowns. Was there any way that Susan could give each boy a signed photo? Susan reached toward the photo box while learning more of the family's story through the lady's tears.

After 17 years of marriage and ministry, her husband had quit both. His departure gutted an unspeakable void in her life and in the hearts of both boys. At about the same time, the family discovered our first album, and the boys particularly latched onto *American Dream*. They even sent their father a copy of the song.

How sad that a child has to "send" his father anything, much less a song that basically begs, "Daddy, please don't. All we really want is you." What leads a man to walk away from everyone he has ever really loved—and certainly everyone who has ever loved him?

I had to shake my head at the story of the tearful mother trying to hold it all together for two little ones because her husband likes the feel of sand between his toes. A little shack on the Rock wasn't good enough.

M

Sandwiched between those stories is a songwriting saga requiring years to canvass. Like the band that works for a decade only to finally break through with a smash hit, *American Dream* was similarly an "overnight success." This was either the second or third song I ever wrote, but I tweaked it through several versions after beginning it in the early 1990s. It has been a double-edged sword. The message is for husbands and fathers everywhere, including me.

Thankfully, I didn't write this song in first person. My dad loved his shack on the rock so much that he also built a shop out back and made sure he took me with him to work among his gaggle of projects—usually in the middle of afternoon cartoons.

My dad was there for me. He worked full-time and overtime for a finance company, high-stress labor in any size town. He was the Andy Griffith of the finance business, always wanting to give more time and more money than clients were due. He wanted to help folks and take chances on them, and people in the corporate world didn't exactly smile on his down-home ways. He would take the grief, deposit it in some secret urn he must've kept in one of his desk drawers, and never, ever would he bring it home to us.

Not even once do I remember wondering, "Hey, where's dad?" I knew where he was, because he was with me—every afternoon playing basketball in the yard or throwing the football in the street. (I'm sure you remember those days—someone yells, "CAR!" and everyone has to scramble to the curb.)

I don't know if dad necessarily enjoyed the same attention as a child, but I know something within him looked at his family and said, "This is the point right here. Everything else is so you can do this." I wish every teenager in my student ministry could live with my parents, because I meet so many kids whose parents don't see their children as blessings. Too many parents scratch through every day to store up what amounts to moth food when their greatest treasure is already under their own roofs, longing for time and affection.

I didn't live out the theme of this song, but I've dealt with it enough as a youth pastor to know that I could best address it through lyrics.

It began as a little piano ballad called *He Works All Day*. The first verse opened with the line, "All work, no play may have made Jack a dull boy" and the second verse followed with, "Not this time, son, I've no time to waste." Those lines remain today, but the verses have evolved over the years. I can still remember the old version because the subject was so gripping to me.

I also remember the first version because it was my pet song for a while and I couldn't stop adding verses to it. I was dangerously close to a nine-minute song, so I had to cut a picturesque verse. Remember, I began writing this song when I was young, so the lost verse doesn't flow perfectly, but here goes:

Took the family out for a picnic,
Got his cell phone at his side;
Middle of the blessing, the phone rings,
Got important people on the line;
The kids start gathering all their toys,
Realizing the day was planned in vain;
Momma's in the car with tears in her eyes,
As it slowly starts to rain.

I liked that verse because it was a day-in-the-life glimpse of the impact of the dad's decisions on his family. But there simply wasn't enough room for it. The song had to resolve, and that verse didn't offer resolution. That's when I remembered the BMW bumper sticker and decided to close with "He used to say whoever dies with the most toys wins."

There were many more changes to come.

The chorus of the original song is now the channel that introduces the chorus and includes an intro line that grows direr as the song progresses:

He works all day and tries to sleep at night...
He works all day and lies awake at night...
He works all day and cries alone at night...

The song's second version was entitled *On Christ I'll Stand.* The new chorus was lifted from the old hymn *The Solid Rock*: "On Christ, the solid Rock I stand/All other ground is sinking sand." So I tried to craft this neat story that segued into the chorus of a famous hymn, a blend of new and old. By then, it had become a sweeping rock song, however, and the boisterous music drowned the message. You took away only the song and not the story.

Time for another change.

We moved to Eagle's Landing, and band member Hector Cervantes shared with me a new guitar riff. We were trying to come up with an idea for the riff but were stuck, so we set it aside as we practiced one night in the gym. We were preparing for our church's annual NASCAR banquet, an evangelism event that would feature Jeff Gordon. We are located in the home county of Atlanta Motor Speedway, and when the spring race hit town, we'd bring in a Christian driver to give his testimony and draw 3,000 people. It was the largest event of its kind in the country, according to the folks who helped us from Motor Racing Outreach.

The band was trying to decide what to play for all of the racing fans when we realized who would be in our audience.

Dads. Hundreds of unchurched dads.

More accustomed to standing before teenagers, we wondered what to communicate. As we went through our song list, I kept thinking, *"Man, that old song about the dad would be awesome."* But the song was just an idea lying dormant in my head. It had never become anything more than a few neat verses sandwiching the chorus of a traditional hymn, and I had not sung that version in years.

It was late. The rest of the band wanted to jam for a little while longer, but I decided to head home. On the interstate, I had Hector's new opening riff stuck in my head and suddenly paired it with the opening lyric to the old dad song: "All work, no play…."

I thought, *"That's cool."*

The words already were written, and I began mentally framing a new melody and Hector's new riff around the old lyrics. Once again, a song came together behind my steering wheel. I got off the interstate, turned around, and called the guys back in the gym. They were packing up when I reached them.

"Don't leave," I said. "I think I've got something."

When I returned and showed them the song, they all agreed: "Dude… this is it!" Hector had another great idea of turning the old chorus into the current channel that introduces the chorus, and I wound up crafting part of the new chorus from the dad's perspective:

But he works…and he builds…with his own two hands…

I sing that one line as the dad would sing it, because in his mind he's doing it all with his own two hands: "I am making my life. I am providing for this family. I'm doing what a man does."

Though the song is biographical, that one line is how he would explain himself. I wanted him to defend himself, because he almost always does in real life. Then the song switches to reality:

And he pours all he has in a castle made with sand;
But the wind and the rain are comin' crashin' in…

I wanted to convey that the dad doesn't see what's coming. When the storms blow in and everything crashes at his feet, he's going to realize it, but it'll be too late. Intentionally, it almost leaves the listener wondering, "Is he ever going to figure this out?" But then the song goes right back into the story.

Two nights later, the first time we played *American Dream* without a mistake was at this huge NASCAR event. At that point, we had never played before a crowd as large, and I still had the old lyrics bouncing around in my head. But we knew NASCAR fans love a good wreck, and we thought the message was worth the risk.

It worked.

Despite all the last-minute wrangling, the song really connected with the dads. In fact, I began receiving letters shortly after that night, most of them with messages similar to the following e-mail:

E-mail: Tuesday, November 23, 2004; 1:12 AM

Thank you for *American Dream.* These lyrics ring so close to a part of my life that it brought tears to my 55-year-old eyes. I pray that young men all over the world hear this message. (Years ago) I was a baby Christian and commuting two hours or more each way to work. Your lyrics tell me that you understand what the time away can do to a family. I remember that one day my son, then six or seven years old, came up to me where I was "collapsed" in my recliner. It was the end of the day and towards the end of the week. I was tired. He had his ball glove and a baseball in his hands. He said, "Hey Dad. You want to play? No, I guess you're too tired, huh?" My heart broke. Jesus used that experience to start one of many changes in my life. He helped me to realize how much more important relationships are. We only get the privilege of experiencing our children once.

I am blessed that both our daughter and son are believers. (Our son) is now the youth group leader at our church. I am also blessed with two grandchildren from our daughter and son-in-law. They are being raised with the attention that my kids should have had. I am also being allowed the opportunity to play a major role in their lives, another blessing.

The message of *American Dream* cannot be told strongly enough or loud enough to the young fathers today. For our children, one of our most valuable assets is *TIME*. What we give, we get back and more.

DGH

Several dads have informed us that God has used the song to inspire them to quit jobs and make complete lifestyle changes to better connect with their kids. Some have said that the only reason they heard about *American Dream* is because one of their kids asked them to listen to the song or to watch the video.

We've been in concerts and seen dads standing with their kids and listening to the music. When we get to *American Dream,* we often see those dads change expressions. You just know God is speaking to them. There is nothing like being onstage and watching the Lord work, because they're just songs until God starts doing something with them in people's hearts. By no means does He need a song to speak to people, but He often speaks through life situations. We have been blessed to see many such situations in which God takes a moment and says, "Pay attention. Listen to this." It is humbling to be onstage and see a father connecting with what's really going on in his family's life—or a daughter standing next to her dad and praying that he does. You can just see the look on her face. It's a powerful moment.

The song reaches across class barriers, too, which intensifies the irony of the BMW lyric:

And then he slips into…his new BMW,
And drives farther and farther and farther away.

I regret using the BMW lyric. I remembered the luxury car with the bumper sticker and wanted to paint the imagery, plus it was a great rhyme. Unintentionally, I may have conveyed the notion that the message pertains only to the affluent. Hardly. This song wears a blue collar just as readily as it does a white one.

No one has room to say, "Well, I don't drive a BMW. I'm just out here trying to work." It's not about the class system or the kind of car.

Sometimes I want to sing that the dad slips into his Ford pickup truck or his Honda Accord. The point is not his being rich. The point is that he's running from relationships that he cannot make happen. Intimacy doesn't come easily for him. When the kids were small, they did what he said or they got into trouble, and that was that. Now that they're teenagers, all of a sudden they have views. They're all geniuses now. And sometimes dad no longer knows how to make the relationship work.

At his job, everybody listens to him. He has input or gives directives and things happen. It's very professional, very clinical. Everything goes through the proper channels, and everything works in that world.

Then he goes home, and it's not the same. There can be no walls or facades in a healthy home. If dad isn't careful, he'll retreat to the world that he can control. Most often, he can control his work life, and even if he cannot, there are rules. Everything is set. There is a boss. There is an employee. There are working hours. There are certain requirements. That kind of sterile structure doesn't exist at home, and dad can easily gravitate back to his controlled, professional world.

That world, by the way, has ready-made rationalizations. When the family confronts dad on his misplaced priorities, he has the handy excuses: "Well, I'm trying to provide for my family," or, "I'm trying to give us a better life." He uses excuses to hide his fear of being a dad at the moment. Or worse—he really doesn't know how to be a dad.

Because his dad lived the American Dream, too.

THE GODLINE

One of the first lines that popped into my head for this song remains one of my favorites. It is sparse but powerful, communicating what is really important for dads—or anyone else—to remember:

> *I'll take a shack on the Rock*
> *Over a castle in the sand.*

That line strikes me because it describes a trade. You cannot have both. You're either going to build your life on Jesus or you're going to build it on the things you think you can control. It's almost the same dilemma described above.

Just as many dads struggle to control their homes, no one controls a relationship with God. We didn't choose Him; He chose us. (John 15:16) It can be difficult to walk this walk—to figure out how it works—and you have to step off of a cliff before you realize that Someone is there to catch you. That's the definition of faith. This world makes much more sense to us. A life of faith is much more foreign to many of us because we haven't truly lived it yet. At least the sand feels familiar. The Rock...sometimes it seems way out there somewhere. It's bumpy and hard and right at water's edge—but it sure makes for a great foundation.

Another line that always sinks its hook into my daddy heart—remember, I have to sing this song several times a week—is the first line of the second verse.

> *Not this time, son; I've no time to waste;*
> *Maybe tomorrow we'll have time to play.*

That verse checks my oil every time I get onstage, and I have to step back and ask myself, "OK, what kind of dad were you today?"

The question isn't, "What kind of dad were you last month?" *Today* is what matters, which is the reason my family travels with me on the road. I refuse to go without them. My commitment prompted me to buy our own family bus. Melanie is the band's road manager, and we homeschool our three kids on the road and at home. We decided shortly after signing our record deal that if it consumes every penny I earn in music for my family to remain together, then so be it. And if we can't, we won't tour.

The day that I have to leave my kids behind is the day I know it's time for me to get off of the road. They come first.

Besides, I hate to feel sand between my toes.

THE BOTTOM LINE

- What kind of dad is/was your father? Can you specify areas in which he impacted your life? For what aspects of his parenting are you grateful? What do you wish he had done differently?
- Are you blaming your father for current issues in your life? Why? For what should you take personal responsibility?
- What kind of a dad (parent) are you? Do you know the name of your child's favorite teacher? Favorite food? Favorite movie? Favorite game? Best friend? Do you know his or her favorite hangout? Favorite music band? Do you know his or her exact daily routine? What grade did he or she make in English last semester? How, specifically, have you been involved in your child's life this week? Today?

CASTINGCROWNS.TV

VIDEO CLIP - "American Dream" from the *Live From Atlanta* DVD You've read it! Now go watch & listen to these stories at www.castingcrowns.tv

Here I Go Again

But how are they to call on him in whom they have not
believed? And how are they to believe in him of whom
they have never heard? And how are they to hear
without someone preaching?

ROMANS 10:14

LAST CHANCE

God reached down and rescued John from the mire. He was a biker
in the Harley vein whose skin was stained with tattoos and whose
life was stained with sin. He wore all the requisite leather, a tough
exterior covering an even more callused interior.

Yet a sovereign Lord looked on His timetable one day and said, "He's one
of Mine," and called John's name. John accepted Jesus and was an instanta-
neous testament to what the Lord meant when He stared at Nicodemus and,
as a nighttime breeze rustled the trees, said:

> *"Truly, truly, I say to you, unless one is born again he cannot see
> the kingdom of God. ...Do not marvel that I said to you, 'You must
> be born again.' The wind blows where it wishes, and you hear its
> sound, but you do not know where it comes from or where it goes. So
> it is with everyone who is born of the Spirit."*
>
> *John 3:3, 7-8*

John had always loved riding the wind, and he wouldn't stop now. He immediately set out on a journey of abandonment. Sometimes you didn't know whether he was coming or going, but, man, could you ever see the leaves shake. I met this sold-out former biker when he and his wife, Jane, were already absorbed in ministry. It was one of those examples in which someone plucked from the darkest of pits now shines the brightest of lights because they have experienced, more than most men, the extent of God's far-reaching grace.

We hit it off because John shared my love of music. He and Jane were troubadours, traveling and writing songs, singing and loving people in the name of Jesus. I met John at school and ministered some with him, and our friendship and families began to grow. We were two men from vastly different backgrounds now united in the same cause; Jesus and music were our glue.

Just as suddenly, I was left shaking my head.

Jane was diagnosed with cancer and died shortly thereafter. At this wind, John was blown away. He didn't know what to believe, and I didn't know what to say. Instead of being abandoned to God, he now felt totally abandoned by God. Some of his old nature kicked in, and John looked heavenward, shrugged, and said, "Fine." And he walked away. I didn't know how to handle it. I had just witnessed the most random, reckless thing I'd ever seen.

There I was, Mr. Christian Pastor Guy with a beautiful marriage and all my hopes and dreams intact, so what could I do? Call him up and say, "Hey John, it's OK. God loves you"? At the time, I thought that was the dumbest thing I'd ever heard. I didn't even know if I believed it anyway.

I was unable to make Jane's funeral halfway across the country. When I phoned John a few times to try to love on him, I struggled to find the right words. In my last conversation with him, he was out there. You could just tell in his voice that he was drained emotionally, physically, and spiritually. I said, "Hey man, how are you doing?"

"I'm tired, just tired" he said, and I could just hear his furrowed brow. He was mad and didn't want to listen to what I had to say.

So I took a deep breath and tried anyway: "Well, I just wanted to let you know I'm praying for you, bro, and we need to get together. Why don't we meet somewhere?" At this point, he was listening only because he was being polite to an old friend.

"Why don't we try to get together soon?" I asked. "I'll just fly you down and you can spend some time with Jeff (a mutual friend) and me."

"Yeah, that sounds like a good idea," he said. "I need to do that."

It never happened. After John drifted away, I tried a few more times to contact him before eventually convincing myself that I really wouldn't be able to find him. It was a convenient excuse. It made me feel better. But I didn't know what else to do.

I also didn't know that in those very moments the Lord was working the first notes of *Here I Go Again* into my life. These notes are sharp and painful, the weightiest of themes. Still, as with our ever-faithful God, they also leave us with hope and put some Harley-sized steel into our souls.

Time was a salve for John. He wrestled with God until he finally met a Christian lady whom God sent to throw out another lifeline. John grabbed hold, returned to church, and began serving again. Life was good, but it certainly wasn't because I had nurtured him back into the fold....

Looking back, I realize I failed my friend.

M

I didn't write *Here I Go Again* with John in mind. But I can't sing it now without thinking of him. It is a song born out of moments such as when I faced John with nothing between us but opportunity and I blew it. Not only did I say little, I did little. I not only shied away but also reasoned it away, which is even worse.

I have heard some comments about how Casting Crowns' music is almost too direct to the Church, that it is as indicting as it is inspiring. If so, it certainly is not because Mr. Perfect fronts the band. A magazine writer said to me one time, "Some people say your music preaches to the choir," the statement phrased almost as if that's a bad thing. My response was, "Yeah, the Bible calls it discipleship."

This is a song of discipleship. But I'm not pointing a finger. I'm looking in a mirror.

Here I Go Again speaks mostly to the person reluctant to share his faith, but it also encompasses those times when we don't really know what to say to someone who is hurting. This is the first song I ever played in which there was complete silence from the audience when I finished. The song just sat there and weighed on everyone, because it's where we all live.

My greatest aim while writing the song was to convey that my intention is not to bash people because they're not speaking forth the truth as they should. A big key to the appeal of this song is that folks know I also struggle with failing to speak forth truth as I should.

So this song is written in first-person for a reason.

The Apostle Paul modeled how to balance mercy and truth. He loved, but he was also transparent. So the message of the song isn't exactly groundbreaking. In 1 Timothy 1:15, Paul is effectively saying, "I'm the chief of sinners. Here's the problem, guys, but I just want you to know that I'm where you are. I've been there too."

In that light, this song is the prayer we offer just before we approach a friend to share our faith—only to shrink away. I wrote the song because I know the prayer well. I'm like Paul. I've been there too.

Maybe this time, I'll speak the words of life
With Your fire in my eyes.
But that old, familiar fear
Keeps tearing at my words.
What am I so afraid of?

What am I so afraid of? That question has no good answer but is infinitely revealing. More than anything, it unearths what we really believe.

Countless times have I stood in the perfect place of the witness and decided that those beautiful shoes didn't fit my bunion feet. (Romans 10:15; Ephesians 6:15) I've been fired up, ready to go, verses on the tip of my tongue—only to let the pounding of my heart drown out God's voice.

In fact, all of us in the Church have been trained well beyond our obedience. We all know the Power Band bracelets with the colored beads. We all know *Steps to Peace with God.* We all know "The Romans Road." We all know the F.A.I.T.H. program or some similar outline. What we obviously do not grasp is an understanding of how God saves people.

I can say I understand it, but my life will reveal what I believe much faster and more profoundly than my words ever will. I can say I believe salvation is all of God, but if that were my belief I'd have no problem sharing my faith. Somewhere between my brain and my heart are some atheistic tendencies. I once heard Pastor Johnny Hunt of First Baptist Church of Woodstock (Georgia) say, "In many areas of our lives we are practical atheists." This song reminds me of his statement. We say, but we don't truly believe. I tell students all the time, "You can say what you think, but you'll live what you believe."

Going further, my brain tells me and Scripture tells me that I'm only watering the seed. (1 Corinthians 3:7) Most likely, all I'm doing is watering a seed someone else planted, and God does the saving. So here is a crucial point that we must work into our hearts and minds: *We cannot save anybody.* I've never saved anyone in my life. I cannot look at a witnessing opportunity and consider myself the person who is going to make or break this eternal moment. I am charged only with loving them like Jesus. God does the heavy lifting. That's what *my brain* tells me and what *Scripture* tells me.

Yet *my life* tells me I obviously don't believe that. Instead, I fear I will say or do something that won't be good enough or strong enough or convincing enough, which is a scary thought—to think I can convince somebody. The consistent evidence suggests that I believe I'm going to do something wrong or prompt too many difficult questions. I think I'm not ready. Consequently, I hold back and don't share. So that means I don't believe what I say. For many of us, it is a source of constant spiritual friction.

We've all walked out of a sermon or a Bible study thinking, *"It's so dumb for me to be scared to do this. That's it. No longer. The next time someone walks up to me, I'll share my faith with him."* Sure enough, the moment soon materializes, our voice cracks, and we silently gasp, *"Oh, no, this is it. I'm not going to say the right thing."* So we don't say anything. In a heavy heartbeat, the moment is gone, the chance has vanished, and we're left defeated because in those moments our faith is not in God. Instead, we improperly place our faith in ourselves.

Another stumbling block also has clipped my witness. It boils down to pride, but it stems from the sobering reality that I probably have not lived for God in front of this person. My fear is that what I share with them will sound so different from my normal behavior and attitude around this person that they're going to look at me and laugh because in their presence I haven't lived the eternal life I'm now professing.

Sometimes we're *afraid* of our faith…
  because it sounds crazy.
    Or we're *ashamed* of our faith…
      Because we haven't been living it.

Usually, at least one of those two concerns gives us pause at a crucial moment. When we should obey Christ and speak forth, we choose instead to shrink back and talk about the high pressure system wafting in from the north. Or maybe we switch gears to sports. Or say or do anything but let the wind blow where it wishes.

All of these shortcomings—a misunderstanding of Scripture, a fear of rejection, and pride—are steeped in some form of fear, which isn't from God anyway. To fear sharing your faith is to misunderstand the Gospel, your role, and God's role.

But Satan slinks in and whispers, *"You're gonna blow this…"* and instantly we're looking back at the waves again. We're not focusing on the Lord and obeying Him.

I've learned all of this through failure, which is a great teacher. I've also learned that it pertains not only to opportunities to share our faith but also to those times when we should reach out to loved ones or friends who have blown it or who are in crisis. Whether it was failing to share the Gospel one on one or simply shying away from sitting with a hurting friend, my life has been an all too familiar refrain when it comes to *Here I Go Again*. There's a scratch on the CD. It just keeps repeating itself.

'Cause here I go again,
Talking 'bout the rain,
And mulling over things
That won't live past today….

I was youth pastor at Center Hill Baptist Church in the early to mid-1990s when I began grappling with this issue. I realized how far short I fell in my personal witness and had worked in the Church long enough to see many others languishing at outreach as well.

On my way back from another family trip to Birmingham, Alabama, I was mulling over how the body of Christ severely struggles in witnessing. A song began percolating. Yet I knew that people would listen to its important message only if I shared frankly and transparently from my personal experiences. I told myself: *"Don't be preachy. Just tell them how I really am."*

The verses came first, as usual. I began humming it and massaging it over the next days and weeks until it took the basic shape of what you hear. I never wrote it down. I debuted it with my Center Hill band, The New Life Rookies, and eventually took it with me to Daytona and introduced it to Casting Crowns. To my knowledge, the first time it ever appeared on paper was in the liner notes of our debut CD. We just always played and sang it by heart. If only I were so faithful with its message....

Who knows?

Maybe John still would be alive.

My friend was planning to re-marry and had rejoined church and the Lord's work. Then one night an old boyfriend of John's new girlfriend showed up with a gun. He shot her dead and then killed himself. John watched it all. When I heard about it, I said, "What is that? God, what's going on?"

John disappeared again. I couldn't find him. Actually, I convinced myself I couldn't find him; the truth is I was just scared to find him. Then someone finally found John. Dead. He had killed himself.

Where is God in all of that? I don't know. I've never totally figured out that one. However, I do know that His redemption continues to thread the story. John and Jane had three kids, into whom they constantly poured truth. That truth didn't die. It wasn't built on John or whether he was around. One of his kids is a youth pastor. Another plays in a Christian band. The other is a little princess and is doing well as a student. They're all between the ages of about 17 and 21, but they were tots when I knew them. I've since re-connected with them, and we've had them at concerts and talked with them on the phone, visiting several times. They are all involved in church, and their grandfather is a pastor.

Out of the chaos, He reigns.

Just consider: Through disease, Satanic attack, doubt, anger, fear, and poor choices, a family was devastated and ministry was sidetracked. And yet the Lord continues to weave healing and restoration—and He does it despite my failures, proving He doesn't need me. He just wants me. My only mission was to throw myself into John's life and love on him. After both tragedies in his life, I failed in some measure. I made more excuses than phone calls. I replaced loving touches with rationalizations. I prayed, "Lord, send John some help," but didn't go. For one reason or another, when it came to trying earnestly to reach out to him, I never pulled the trigger....

And then he did.

THE GODLINE

I've gotten dozens of letters and e-mails from people who were emboldened to share their faith simply from one line in this song, which is why I know it's the Godline. There's no way it came from me.

> *And as I dance around the truth,*
> *Time is not his friend.*
> *This might be my last chance*
> *To tell him that You love him.*

Some people have told me, "I finally had to share with my dad right before he died." I've gotten several e-mails from people inspired to share their faith with someone who was near death. They all say something like, "I was so scared, but I realized this might be the last chance." That's the line they always reference in their correspondence, like this one:

E-mail: Thursday, January 06, 2005; 4:40 PM

I just wanted to share with you what a huge blessing your lyrics are to me. My best friend had no relationship with Christ at all and I have been praying for him for years. He knew where my heart is and we had discussions, but it wasn't until I heard *Here I Go Again* that I realized I had to do something before it's too late.

When I first heard that song, I was in tears and I knew that God was using the song to speak to my heart. Long story short, my friend has accepted Christ as his Lord and Savior, and the funny thing is that after

we finished praying I shared with him why I felt "now" was the time. I
put your CD in, and instead of *Here I Go Again* (which is what I intended
to play for him) I accidentally pushed Track Five, *American Dream,* and
by the time the song was over he was moved to tears. He is a very
successful man whose dad was never home and whose mom was
less than loving, and he told me years ago that he would never be that
way. Well, *American Dream* came on and he realized at that moment
he was the guy in the song who didn't have time for his kids or his
wife, even down to the new BMW that he purchased just days earlier.
I thank you for sharing your gift with the rest of us. Because of your
music, not only is my best friend saved but he has switched jobs so
that he can be with his family, and he is no longer traveling or working late. I am sure there are many stories like this one out there, but I
really wanted to thank you from the bottom of my heart for making
music that is Spirit-led and that not only ministers to the unsaved but
really speaks to the heart of the Body of Christ as it encourages and
convicts us to act now before it's too late. May God continue to use
you and bless you.
Carter K.

Obviously, God deserves all praise for saving this man's soul and changing
his heart, but I am humbled to hear the Lord used one of our songs in His
plan.

I think one of the song's strongest moments comes toward the end, when
I repeat the Godline three times with increasing emphasis. *This might be my
last chance to tell him that You love him.* The music gets louder each time, and
it's communicating that this *really* might be the last chance.

I've tried to tell John's story about four times in concert, but I've never been
able to finish. I just have to start singing. I remember my last conversation
with John. At the time, I didn't know that was it. I was probably thinking,

"Maybe this is setting up for the day that I'll be able to say something spiritual and fix all of this."

Nope. It was *the last time.*

THE BOTTOM LINE

- Name the one person whom you most wish God would save. When was the last time you witnessed to that person?

- As you think about lost loved ones and friends, rate the importance of the following elements as you prepare to share with them: A) evangelism training; B) apologetics research; C) prayer; D) Scripture memorization; E) proper perspective of your role and God's role; F) reliance upon the Holy Spirit. Explain your ordering of these priorities.

- Write down the name of the person you most wish God would save. Will you make a commitment to witness to him or her (not a commitment to invite him or her to church, but to present the Gospel) within the next week?

- Today's date: _____

CASTINGCROWNS.TV

VIDEO CLIP - "Here I Go Again" from the *Live From Atlanta* DVD
You've read it! Now go watch & listen to these stories at
www.castingcrowns.tv

Praise You with the Dance

Let them praise his name with dancing...
PSALM 149:3

LAWNMOWER SONG

I can't remember his name or his church, but I probably could find my copy of the cassette tape if you pressed me for it.

I cannot forget his story, however.

Someone gave me a recording of an incredible moment in the life of an evangelist whom, for some reason, God sidelined for a while. The evangelist developed a throat disease that silenced him. All he could produce was a coarse whisper. He lost his voice, but he never lost his passion for Jesus or for God's Word, and he was considered a terrific Bible teacher. Undaunted, he left the road, plugged into his church, and started teaching a Sunday School class. A microphone amplified his whisper and also allowed for weekly taping, which is the only reason I'm able to share this story—because I heard it myself.

The former evangelist taught for a few years, remaining faithful when many would've become bitter. I've thought about this man often, wondering how he maintained his faith and positive attitude when his preferred ministry was taken from him. What would I do if I lost my voice, if I couldn't sing? Would I retire to my church and remain faithful in the ministry? I hope I would. I believe I would. But here was a man who did.

I listened to the cassette as he preached on Psalm 103 and read aloud Verses 2-4.

Bless the LORD, O my soul,
And forget not all his benefits,
Who forgives all your iniquity,
Who heals all your diseases,
Who redeems your life from the pit,
Who crowns you with steadfast love and mercy…

The teacher's class was quiet as he read aloud in his whisper, "Who heals all your diseases." He paused and said, "You know, I don't know why He does this, but He does. Some of us He chooses not to heal, and some us He chooses to heal, but that's His sovereign choice."

He returned to the passage and continued reading, whispering the next line, "Who redeems your life FROM THE PIT." Instantly, his voice returned in mid-sentence. He spoke the words "from the pit" in full voice. It startled him. He paused and repeated himself, still in full voice: "Who redeems…your life…from the pit." There is no other sound on the tape. The class is stunned and completely silent.

The once-and-future evangelist seems almost fearful: "I don't…know what's happening…right now.…" Someone in the class yelps in glee, "Woooo!" And the rest of the class comes unglued. They go nuts, and I was left with goosebumps and a grin as I stared at the tape player. The evangelist finished the entire lesson in his normal voice, and it's all on tape. It was one of the most powerful moments I've ever experienced, and that verse stuck with me.

In so many ways, Jesus has redeemed my life from the pit. He wanted me when I didn't want Him, and He pulled me out of the pit when I was unable to escape on my own.

M

One of the blessings of my youth pastorate at Center Hill Baptist was the use of the church parsonage and the church lawnmower, which came in handy considering the parsonage's front and back yards. The back yard was connected to the church's softball field, which, thankfully, I did not have to mow. Still, the acreage was large enough that I called it my "Back 40," and it required substantial time on the riding mower. It was a songwriter's dream.

That's where my "Lawnmower Song" was born; it's titled *Praise You with the Dance* on our first CD.

The parsonage was nestled in pretty countryside surrounded by tall pines and robust hardwoods, and every time I fired up the mower I couldn't help but feel my smallness in God's vastness. So I would start singing this little worship song that kept bouncing around in my head. Cars zoomed past on the highway, their drivers laughing at the guy bellowing from the top of his lungs, but I didn't care. I saw God's beauty and it reminded me of my wretchedness, and I couldn't help but remember the old evangelist whose raspy voice grew strong as God reassured him that He had redeemed his life from the pit. I knew the feeling, so the words of Psalm 103 and Psalm 40 helped frame this worship song. Psalm 40:1-2 states:

> *I waited patiently for the LORD;*
> *he inclined to me and heard my cry.*
> *He drew me up from the pit of destruction,*
> *out of the miry bog,*
> and set *my feet upon a rock,*
> *making my steps secure.*

In the spirit of the healed evangelist, the first verse of the song proclaims that I will sing to the Lord and "lift my voice." The second verse concludes with a praise: "For You have brought me out of the pit."

Satan still tries to dampen my enthusiasm on occasion: "Why are you doing this? You don't deserve to do this. You are a sorry dog to stand up here and try to sing these songs to Him." It helps to remind myself that those people who have been forgiven much are the ones who should sing even louder. If ever you see me choked up, especially in the middle of a worship song, it's because I'm remembering the truths of Psalms 103 and 40 and I realize just how far He reached down to yank me out of that pit. The New Testament puts it this way:

> *He has delivered us from the domain of darkness and transferred us to the kingdom of his beloved Son, in whom we have redemption, the forgiveness of sins.*
>
> *Colossians 1:13-14*

So I wanted my "Lawnmower Song" to create a happy time, and people always have embraced its upbeat rhythm because it gives us permission to be giddy over Jesus. Some people may harrumph at the notion, but I see throughout the Bible examples of being given permission—whether you're a good Baptist or not—to dance over the Lord. David danced in 2 Samuel 6:13-15, and the following song was sung at the dedication of the Temple of David:

> *You have turned for me my mourning into dancing; you have loosed my sackcloth and clothed me with gladness, that my glory may sing your praise and not be silent. O LORD my God, I will give thanks to you forever!*
>
> *Psalm 30:11-12*

I usually place *Praise You with the Dance* somewhere within the first several songs of our concert playlist. It so frees the atmosphere, especially after we've delivered a couple of heavy-hitting songs touching on several serious topics, that people seem to be more inclined to sincerely worship afterward. It centers the focus upon Jesus and not on us or what we do.

Melodee DeVevo's violin solo, in which she samples the song *Simple Gifts,* is a great interlude inviting people to let loose and worship. They can clap their hands, sit down, close their eyes and pray, dance—whatever they want to do. It is unique for a worship song to avail the opportunity to worship without singing. Usually we're telling you what to do the whole song: *Read this, say this, and sing these notes like this.* But we decided to create a moment in which people could worship God as they saw fit, whatever dance means to them. Just like David. That embarrasses the Michals out there (2 Samuel 6:16), but we've seen people lock arms and go around in a circle; we've seen people lift their hands; we've seen people just watch and say, "Look at that nut." I'm thankful for a God who has blessed us with such simple gifts, and I believe it's perfectly fine to get a little giddy about Jesus.

After all, Verse 1 of Psalm 40 states that He heard my cry, and Verse 2 tells us that He lifted us out of a slimy pit. Guess what Verse 3 proclaims?

He put a new song in my mouth, a song of praise to our God.

Even on a lawnmower.

THE GODLINE

There is one reason this song exists. There is one reason I worshipped the Lord and wrote this song while cutting grass. There is one reason I still cry when I think about His grace: I love to sing back to Him that one reason:

For You have brought me out of the pit.

That Godline is the reason I can sing. I sing to Jesus not because one day I realized I was living a bad life and decided I needed to turn over a new leaf. I sing to Jesus not because I followed 12 steps to peace or completed any other program.

God reached into the pit I dug with my own hands, opened my eyes to the realization I was down there, and pulled me out. There is so much of my salvation that He arranged and performed—and I have so little to do with it—that it just makes me want to worship Him even more.

Many believers assume they somehow initiated a relationship with God, which creates misunderstanding in many areas. Think about it: If I created this moment, I can un-create this moment. If I began this relationship, I can end it. If I did something that connected me with God, I can possibly do something that will disconnect me from Him. No, we must remember that when were dead in our trespasses, God reached down, enlightened us, quickened our spirits, gave us the gifts of faith and the Holy Spirit, and yanked us out of deep garbage.

There are days in which, for some inexplicable reason, I attempt to drag Him back through that garbage, but He always pulls me out. It's not my grip on Him that matters; it's His grip on me. I did nothing to make Him love me, and I can't do anything to make Him stop.

It's enough to make me want to praise Him. Maybe even with a little dance.

THE BOTTOM LINE

- When was the last time you were awestruck at the majesty and splendor of our loving Lord? Remember and recite the specifics as an act of worship.
- Why do we miss God so often when His work is so abundant? What helps you slow down and see God for who He is? What is keeping you from doing so right now?
- Can you recall an instance when you saw God move miraculously? What were the circumstances? Did you offer Him thanks and praise at the time? Have you ever shared the story to give Him praise? Are you willing to share the story again soon?

Glory

Then I looked, and I heard around the throne and the
living creatures and the elders the voice of many
angels, numbering myriads of myriads and thousands
of thousands, saying with a loud voice, "Worthy is the
Lamb who was slain, to receive power and wealth and
wisdom and might and honor and glory and blessing!"
REVELATION 5:12

HIS RIGHTEOUS
RIGHT HAND

I should have known this would be a special worship song; I could feel the
hand of God moving, but I couldn't feel my own.

That I could even play the piano was proof enough that the Lord was
involved.

Huey Long had to have possessed one of the strongest grips in Georgia.
I'm not certain, but I believe he was a farmer. What I do know is he worked
with his hands. A lot. Huey wasn't the reason that Pastor David Dills called
our Monday night men's prayer meetings the "Power Hour," but it would not
have been a stretch. I remember eventually learning from experience and
scouting whom I would stand beside in the prayer circle each week. If it was
Huey, I'd either move or start praying a little early.

The Power Hour became an anchor for about 15 men at Center Hill

Baptist Church just outside of Atlanta. It was my first job after graduation from college. Before Center Hill, I had worked as a part-time music and youth pastor for just over a year at New Zion Baptist Church outside of Bonifay, Florida and then in the same roles for three years at Samson (Alabama) First Baptist. I was a full-time student while working both of those jobs. My first three years as a full-time youth pastor were at Center Hill in Loganville, Georgia before I moved to First Baptist Church of Daytona Beach for about two-and-a-half years. I'm now in my fourth year at Eagle's Landing First Baptist Church in McDonough, Georgia, another Atlanta suburb.

Throughout my calling, the Power Hour has remained among my fondest memories. We enjoyed a devotional led by Pastor David, followed by a prayer time as we circled the altar and pulpit. We grabbed hands and asked the Lord to grab our hearts. We prayed for each other, for our families, for what God was doing there and that we wouldn't do anything to get in His way. The prayers were so different because each man was so unique, and it was beautiful.

Then there was Huey. If you stood next to him, you knew that during the prayer you were going to lose all feeling in your hand. Yet his prayers were always among the Power Hour's most profound, Spirit-filled moments. He was so godly. He was a strong man who loved Jesus and loved our church, and one of the reasons I came was just to hear him pray. I was among a handful of young men who had absolutely nothing to offer the group. We were just gleaning whatever we could from pillars like Huey. In the middle of one of those Monday night prayers, I was standing there listening and praying when it began to flow—not the blood in my hand, but a melody. And then these words.

You are holy in this place;
You are worthy of my praise and we worship You.
Jesus, we worship You.

It suddenly popped into my head, the words and the music almost simultaneously arriving. Silently, I began singing it while we were praying.

When we said "Amen" that night, I walked about 15 feet to the piano and, with the men gathered around me, played it for the first time off the top of my head. That brief verse sparked a song that I would title *Holy is the Lord*. Shortly afterward, we began using it in worship on Sunday mornings and Sunday nights, and it became something of a special song for us, especially with Pastor David having witnessed how it started.

The chorus was the same as it is now, except I also included the line, "Holy, holy, holy is the Lord." The song became a worship staple for me at Center Hill and Daytona Beach, where I met Hector Cervantes, one of our guitarists in Casting Crowns. After we formed our band in Daytona, Hector told me he was working on a worship song idea. He already had words for one part:

When You call my name, I'll run to You,
I'll do anything You ask me to;
Falling on my knees I worship You, my Lord
We give You GLORY!

We were in the basement of my house one night working on a few ideas when *Glory* came together. We took Hector's great ideas and melded them with my early version called *Holy is the Lord,* and I easily deposited my original words into his new melody. The Lord has used the result in countless worship times at two different churches and in concerts around the country.

Like most songs, *Glory* is a conglomeration of multiple ideas and influences. First, I thank the Lord for giving me the original idea in the middle of prayer time. But I also can thank Hector, who knows how much I love and appreciate him, and Huey Long, a giant but gentle man who probably doesn't realize what a blessing he continues to be in my life.

Reflecting upon that night during the Power Hour, I realize that only the Lord had a stronger grip than Huey. It also reminds me of two tremendous passages. The first is Psalm 20:6:

Now I know that the LORD saves his anointed; he will answer
him from his holy heaven with the saving might of his right hand.

The second passage comes from Oswald Chambers' devotional book *My Utmost for His Highest*:

"Who are the people who have influenced us most? Certainly not the ones who thought they did, but those who did not have even the slightest idea that they were influencing us. In the Christian life, godly influence is never conscious of itself. If we are conscious of our influence, it ceases to have the genuine loveliness which is characteristic of the touch of Jesus. We always know when Jesus is at work because He produces in the commonplace something that is inspiring."[1]

To the world, Huey may be considered a common man. To me, he was inspiring.

THE GODLINE

This one is obvious. The Godline, the line I'm certain God gave me, is the opening verse that came to me during the Power Hour.

You are holy in this place;
You are worthy of my praise and we worship You.
Jesus, we worship You.

However, another lyric is equally powerful simply for its grand truth. The chorus reads:

You're the King of kings and Lord of lords;
You're the Master of the universe;
You're the Ruler of all nations,
And we sing to You.

Think about the pronouncements of that chorus. I know I have. One day, I had a refreshing yet humbling epiphany: *God, we get to sing to You. Amazingly, inexplicably, undeservedly, we get to sing to You, the King of kings and Lord of lords!*

It's not that we *must* sing to God. Instead, we get the *privilege* of singing to Him, and He hears us. He hears us because He desires to enjoy a relationship and fellowship with us. Wherever I am—in an arena of 10,000 people or at a piano surrounded by a dozen men in a little country church outside of Loganville, Georgia—God, the Master of the universe, the Ruler of all nations, hears me as I sing to Him.

What a reason to give Him *Glory!*

THE BOTTOM LINE

- When was the last time you recognized that God had answered a specific prayer or suddenly had moved on your behalf? What was your response? How did you feel? What impact did it have on your perspective of God and your relationship with Him?
- How do you view worship—as an obligation or a privilege? Is that view reflected in how you worship?
- Think of the believers who have most influenced your life. How did they impact you? Did they realize their impact? Have you ever told them and thanked them?

And let the peace of Christ rule in your hearts, to
which indeed you were called in one body. And be
thankful. Let the word of Christ dwell in you richly,
teaching and admonishing one another in all wisdom,
singing psalms and hymns and spiritual songs,
with thankfulness in your hearts to God.
And whatever you do, in word or deed,
do everything in the name of the Lord Jesus,
giving thanks to God the Father through him.
COLOSSIANS 3:15-17

GOD IMITATORS

One of my many discoveries in ministry is the power of the question. Few approaches have the ability to cut through the maze and haze of life as does simply asking questions, and it has helped me write songs, lead worship, teach sermons, counsel hurting teens, and shape my worldview.

I believe the art of questioning is one of the surest ways of examining my walk with Christ. I look at God's Word—the plumb line—and then I look at where I am and where I'm headed, and I begin asking questions. If something doesn't square with God's Word, it takes about a nanosecond to figure that out. I may spend the rest of the time rationalizing or trying to squirm out of the inevitable conclusion produced by conviction, but usually there is little ambiguity after my questions have invited God's answers.

There is a reason Hebrews 4:12-13 states that the Word of God is sharper than any two-edged sword; not only do we wield it as the sword of the Spirit in spiritual warfare (Ephesians 6:17), but we also benefit from the backside of the blade filleting us wide open, leaving us uncovered and laid bare before Him to whom we must give account. God has no questions and doesn't need them. We do.

As a result, Ephesians 5:1-2 is one of my favorite verses. It is the first verse we listed as a theme verse for *Life of Praise* in the album's liner notes:

> *Be imitators of God, therefore, as dearly loved children and live a life of love, just as Christ loved us and gave himself up for us as a fragrant offering and sacrifice to God. (NIV)*

If we are to live a life of praise, we must be imitators of God—not imitators of the pastor, the head of the deacons, the well-dressed businessman at the end of the pew, or the lady up front who always raises her hands in worship, apparently sensing something we must be missing. A life of praise is authentic. It is personal. It is unmistakably stamped with the seal of the King of the universe. There is no doubt to Whom a person living a life of praise is surrendered.

Unfortunately, there is little doubt that a real life of praise is far too rare these days. This sobering truth is what I walked into when I became youth pastor at First Baptist Church of Daytona Beach in 1997. Out of that experience, this song was born.

I stood before a great group of kids each week. I loved the church and had a powerful sense of God's call to that particular ministry, yet I instantly learned they had never discovered worship. To those kids, worship was merely singing time before the message. So I dove into this issue, which, incidentally, also plagues many adult congregations.

Guess how I approached the situation. I asked questions. I asked them aloud—to leaders and to students. I questioned myself. I questioned our intentions and our motives. Repeatedly, I looked from the stage and simply asked, "Why are we doing this? If what we're singing and saying in here is not coming out of our lives at all, then what is this?"

It was trial-by-fire accountability, which can be uncomfortable, like the adolescent whose bones grow faster than his ligaments care to give. Yet I was determined to convey and reach one goal: "Hey, we need to match what we're singing here."

Why be so insistent on the point? Because the only reason I could identify this shortcoming in the lives of those students is because I've seen it in my own life before. I've stood in worship and mindlessly read the words on the screen and let them pass through my lips without filtering them through my heart. Brain worship. It's safe, it's easy, and it's 18 inches from life change.

As an aside, I believe this same principle—seeing something so clearly in others' lives because you've seen it in your own life—is what makes sin easy to spot in other people's lives. I don't immediately recognize people who have a bent toward gambling because I've never struggled with that before, but I can spot somebody who is bitter a mile away. I usually can sense when someone is numbed by church or when someone is not really walking with God during the week. I can identify these folks because I know what I look like when I do the same. When I walked into my Daytona youth group, I saw myself all over the room, and I needed to give them a loving shake. I had to say, "Hey, let me tell you what happens to me when I'm not living what I'm singing."

So I told them. I told them there are two ways of living—the broad, easy way or the difficult, narrow way. (Matthew 7:13-14) Only the latter leads to genuine worship. Only the latter produces a life of praise.

BROAD IS THE GATE...

The average church is filled with people who live on Broad Street. I know the lay of the land, so let me give you directions out of it.

When I'm not living for Jesus daily and show up at church after squeezing out life on my own terms all week, I'm needy when I walk through the doors.

- I need the greeter to make me feel welcome.
- I need my friend to sit by me.
- I need the soloist to sing my favorite song.
- I need the pastor to be engaging.
- I need the small group leader to love on me and do cartwheels when I enter.
- I need the small group care leader to call me when I'm sick.

I am so needy because I'm not complete when I get there, and when I'm not being completed by my walk with Jesus, I unwittingly demand completeness from people. I raise the bar of expectations, and people don't meet my needs because it is impossible for people to do so.

Then I also face a Catch-22. When I'm not walking with Jesus during the week and then come to church I'm reminded of just how wide the chasm has grown. Why sing when I'm so far away from God that He couldn't possibly hear me? Why worship when nothing comes out of a heart full of…nothing?

This scenario usually produces one of two results: I experience godly sorrow that generates repentance (2 Corinthians 7:10), or I callus over and turn my attention elsewhere. I find items to read in the weekly bulletin. I notice what others are wearing. I think about the afternoon's football matchups. I arrange lunch preparations in my head. Sound familiar? Have you ever done that?

Have you ever pursued those little escape moments to remove yourself, as much as possible, from the thought that something is not right in your life? Sometimes our little escapes even include dwelling upon what's wrong in somebody else's life—what's wrong with the guy three rows back who everybody knows is an alcoholic, or what's wrong with the pastor's presentation, or what's wrong with the day's music selection. It takes half of the Sunday service to get our minds and spirits engaged, and by then worship is over. We pantomimed another week.

Can't you just see the screen with the words to the worship songs? They have such grandiose statements: "You are the Lord of my life"…"You are all I need"…"You are my everything." Such terrific claims!

I am left wondering whether we even hear what we're saying when we repeat such lyrics. I confess that I have been in the middle of worship, paused, looked at the words on the screen that I had been merely reciting, and thought, *"Wow, I haven't lived like that at all this week."*

It all stems from not walking day by day and moment by moment with Jesus.

NARROW IS THE ROAD…

Conversely, when I faithfully pursue God, spending time with Him in Bible study and a spirit of unceasing prayer, then I'm completed by Him. He indeed is all I need. Somehow, Sunday shifts places within the week. It is no longer the last and merely dutiful day of the weekend before another mundane Monday. Instead, it's the first day of a new week of new life. It is first-fruits to God. When I walk into church, I see people like He sees them. I see others as people who need to see the love of Jesus through me. In other words, I recognize and acknowledge that I'm an instrument. I walk in and want to sit by others as a ministry. I want to help greet visitors. I want to make sure somebody called those who were sick. Why? Because a life of praise comes from understanding that this life is not about us. It's about something bigger than us. It's about loving God and loving others, the two greatest commandments. (Matthew 22:35-40)

That's why I wrote this song. I had asked so many questions of my youth group in Daytona, and now I was asking for authenticity. I just put the answers to music.

I wrote the opening verse first, and, to me, its words say it all:

I will love You, Lord, always,
Not just for the things You've done for me.

And I will praise You all my days,
Not just for the change You've made in me.

The message is clear: I'm not praising a Santa Claus god. Rather, I'm praising Him for who He really is, which inherently requires that I know and understand who He is. Then it is only natural to praise God for who He is and not for what He can do for me. Out of a heart of resounding gratitude, I live a life of praise.

Believe me, people are watching. They are longing for something real, and they reservedly sit back and check to see whether our actions honor or forsake our words. Last summer, a fellow reminded me of just how powerfully God uses a life of praise to impact His kingdom and our world:

E-mail: Thursday, June 23, 2005; 2:31 PM

Dear Casting Crowns:

First off, I want to say you have great music and a wonderful message that you all promote.

The primary reason I am writing is to tell you that you came to my town of Cookeville, Tennessee, some time last year. I took my lost friend, whom for the past year I was trying to lead to Christ, to the concert. After the concert, he asked me what you were talking and singing about. I told him, and he accepted Christ as his Savior. The following week, he told me that he was moving up north. Three days after he moved, he was in an awful car wreck and subsequently died. He was 16 years old. I intended to write you sooner, but I had put it off until I saw you last night at the Southern Baptist Convention when I was 20 feet away from the band.

So thank you for being in my area when you were, because now I know that my friend died with Jesus in his heart and a better home to go to.

From one brother to another,
Joe G.

THE GODLINE

It is not a coincidence that *Life of Praise,* the last original song on the first album, features themes that carry over into the second album: Living a *Life of Praise* is nothing more than letting your *Lifesong* sing, and the picture of hands raised in worship surfaces in both songs. There is a reason.

In fact, the Godline for this song includes the hands theme:

But I'll praise You, for You are holy, Lord
And I'll lift my hands, but You are worthy of so much more.

The first song on our second album is *Lifesong,* and the first line of that song is: *Empty hands held high/Such small sacrifice.* The songs *Stained Glass Masquerade* and *Father, Spirit, Jesus* on the second album also feature the hands theme, because worship must be more than just singing. It's more than just standing and clapping along in a big room. And it's more than just raising your hands. Worship must come out in my heart, in my hands, in my feet, in my workaday life. Or it's not sincere.

Look back at Ephesians 5:1-2, which gives two instructions. Not only are we to be imitators of God, but we also are to live a *life of love.* Exactly. When we imitate a holy God, we live a life of love. We live a life of praise.

THE BOTTOM LINE

- In your own words, write down a simple definition of what it means to be an "imitator of God." Now, honestly assess your walk with Jesus: How seriously do you take the charge to be an imitator of God? How does this show up in your life?

- The importance of the fundamental disciplines of prayer and Bible study cannot be overstated in the believer's life. OK, so how faithful are you? How would you rate your prayer life right now, and how do you think it could improve? How consistent are you in studying God's Word? Do you have a systematic approach? Are you willing to determine to improve? How?

- Do you consider yourself a servant of the Lord and of others? In what ways are you a servant? Conversely, you may be willing to freely give of yourself—many folks don't mind laboring in the Lord's name—but have you truly ever received anything from Him? If you have not received His forgiveness of sins personally, then you have not experienced His salvation. A believer with a humble servant's heart is someone who knows that God doesn't need him but that he needs God. Have you truly received His humiliating offering? Or instead of being an imitator of God, are you trying to be an *imitation* of Him?

"Have I not commanded you?
Be strong and courageous. Do not be frightened,
and do not be dismayed, for the LORD your God
is with you wherever you go."
JOSHUA 1:9

PHONE CALLS
AND FRIENDS

I went through about a week of weirdness.

I'm not sure how else to describe what I experienced while preparing to record our second album. We were coming off of our debut CD, which featured many of the best songs we had worked on for years. Then, all of a sudden, it was time to produce a second album. That meant more new songs; I still had some I had been kicking around for months or years, but most were unfinished.

Some songs I would start from scratch. Some I would completely remake. Others I simply would tweak.

I went to Nashville and settled in for a few weeks to nail down all these ideas flitting through my brain. I discovered that Music City has some lonely streets between First and Second. First albums can be fun. You've had your entire life to pour into them. Second albums, I learned, can be brutal. The first album that was so fun now becomes the standard by which so many people measure you. And the second album can quickly become an albatross.

If you let it.

I teamed again with my friend Mark Miller, who produced our debut CD, and headed back into the studio. We recorded the title track *Lifesong* without any trouble. The song came together perfectly; the music was awesome and sufficiently projected the message's punch. We returned the second day to begin recording some of my other ideas. They were all just bouncing around in my head and I had never heard the completed versions out loud before. When the recording light went on, however, I suddenly didn't like what I was hearing. I tried to be a good soldier and march ahead, but I kept thinking, *"Oh, no. This isn't right."*

The music was running away with many of the songs. They were becoming more about the music than the message, which is totally opposite of my philosophy. The music is supposed to be only a tool, a platter upon which the message is served. It's not the point. If it becomes the point, you are left with only noise. *Lifesong* was perfectly balanced, but now all the other song's lyrics were drowning in waves of sound.

After about a week, I grew uneasy and started thinking: *"This isn't going well. I don't know what this means."*

I never sensed pressure from other people. No one ever questioned where we were headed with the record. No one, that is, but me. I was pressuring myself, and I can only assume I was letting a little flesh get in the way.

Right about that time, the Lord sent me some friends.

My cell phone rang. Mac Powell from Third Day was on the other end.

"Hey man, I hear you're up in the studio," Mac said. "How's it going?"

"Man, I don't know. They sounded way better in my head than they do now."

Mac didn't hesitate.

"Dude, you just need to say what you know God wants you to say and don't take your eyes off of that," he said. "Keep your eyes on what God wants you to say and just say it."

The very same week, Steven Curtis Chapman and I were hanging out when I shared how halting the process had become. Once again, God echoed the same message.

"Man, I've been in the same boat you're in," Steven said. "When it's just you and God, everything makes sense, but when everybody else starts hearing it, they don't even have to say anything but you start thinking, *I wonder if this person likes it,*' or, *'I wonder what he thinks about it.'* Pretty soon, you're changing things because of that. You've got to back up and ask yourself some hard questions. What does God want to say through this? You've got to say what He wants you to say."

Message received.

Those two conversations with mentors whom I respect left me with the very conclusion I believe the Lord had intended:

> *"God, You know what You want to say. I just don't want to mess it up. So I'm dropping this in Your lap."*

From then on, the remainder of the songs gradually changed. A sure sign that God was moving came when a few of the songs I had feared most and others I was most unimpressed with became my favorite songs. I had grappled with *Does Anybody Hear Her?* for years. In fact, half of it was written in the late 1990s when I was youth pastor at Center Hill Baptist Church. I had never nailed down the song, however, and it had become such a comfortable unfinished project that I always referred to it as "The Girl Song." Out of habit, I still do.

Stained Glass Masquerade was another song that went from labor to love because God gently formed it into what He intended for it to be. Most of this didn't involve me at all.

By the end of that worrisome week, the songs blossomed and the notes began to flow. I had to re-learn that I'm not the focal point. Basically, I had to be reminded of everything that I've ever preached about God: He doesn't need us. He wants us.

It was time to *let* my lifesong sing. I had to allow it to happen. That means I had to get out of God's way.

THE GODLINE

I know I received direction from the Lord during this difficult window of songwriting before our second album. It wasn't a lyric. It was an admonition.

"Keep your eyes on what God wants you to say and just say it."

Two different friends whom I know to be godly men offered me the same message at different times. Sometimes the Lord chooses to speak through His Word. Sometimes He speaks through circumstances. And sometimes He speaks through others. The caveat is you have to be sure that those people to whom you are listening are truly walking with God, and their counsel always must square with Scripture. If it doesn't, ignore it.

But this came from Mac Powell and Steven Curtis Chapman.

I'll take it.

THE BOTTOM LINE

- Have you ever gotten in God's way and eventually hampered His work when everything had been going well? Think about those circumstances for a moment and write out a brief description of the events. Afterward, record the lessons you learned and reference any Scripture God used to cement that lesson.
- How often do you seek counsel from people whom you know to be

godly and consistent in their walks with Jesus? Read Proverbs 11:14 and 15:22. Now read Proverbs 13:20. How highly does God view your dependence on godly relationships? Why?

- Read James 5:16. What does this verse mean? Do you have a fellow believer who helps hold you accountable to God's Word? Or do you feel uncomfortable with the notion? Why? On the other hand, sometimes God wants you to share truth with others. Has the Lord ever brought you to a place in a relationship where you had to decide whether your friendship was more important to you than what God wanted you to tell him or her? Sometimes your friend needs truth more than he or she needs a buddy. Has God ever led you to share truth with someone else? Were you obedient? What was the outcome? Regardless of the outcome, do you feel like you honored the Lord?

Lifesong

For those whom he foreknew he also predestined
to be conformed to the image of his Son, in order that
he might be the firstborn among many brothers.
ROMANS 8:29

MAKING JESUS SMILE

The sky was stunning as it draped the wide-open spaces above the HiFi Buys Amphitheatre in Atlanta, providing a picturesque canopy for a worshipful evening.

Third Day was onstage, and as youth pastor at Eagle's Landing First Baptist Church I had my youth group assembled on blankets about midway back on the grassy knoll of this open-air venue just south of Atlanta. The amphitheatre is only about 20 miles from Eagle's Landing, so we took quite a contingent to hear Third Day play before a huge crowd in its hometown.

Casting Crowns was yet to be "discovered." The irony has since struck me: After our first album was released and we began playing concerts, I got to know the guys in Third Day, particularly singer Mac Powell. As I shared in the previous chapter, Mac's encouraging phone call helped me persevere through the difficult process of writing our second album. I can't remember if I told him, but my experience at one of his concerts a few years earlier had sparked the title track to the very *Lifesong* album he eventually encouraged me to finish.

The concert was particularly worshipful. Brilliant stars punched out of the night sky, the environment making it easy to see God for who He is—and to see myself for who I really am. At one point, I noticed that everyone around me had their hands raised in worship. I did too. About halfway through a song, I realized I hadn't walked with Jesus that day. I had not honored Him in the least with how I had handled situations and spent my time and gifts. I had lived more for myself than for Him.

So my worship time that night quickly bogged down into a confessional. My prayer was, "God, please forgive me for how I've lived my day." It should have been, "God, I give You glory." In fact, I'm guilty of this far too often. My moments of worship often include repentance instead of strictly giving God glory because I have to bundle it all into one moment.

I believe this is why Sunday mornings in America are so muted. Where passion belongs, there is only guilty formality. Where transparency should prevail, facades do. Where abandonment is required, only tepid reservation is present. There is a reason.

Sunday morning spit baths are not sufficient to help us survive the cesspool that is this world. All the spiritual gunk we carry into church comes from a week spent more in the world than in the Word. It's impossible to live a Spirit-filled, God-driven life when the only time surrendered to Jesus is an hour-long slot before lunch every other Sunday. How can a person genuinely worship a holy, holy, holy God under such circumstances? Everything has to happen in 30 minutes of worship. Many times I have to get cleaned up first before I can give glory to God. What I should be doing is overflowing with praise from having honored God with my life all week.

I stop short of saying that my hands were raised at the Third Day concert only because everyone else's hands were in the air. I remember looking up at my hands, seeing the sky above, and realizing how huge it was in comparison. Then it hit me.

"My hands have not been holy today. These aren't holy hands offered to a holy God. They're just empty hands."

My empty hands were not saying what I was singing. It is easy to mouth the words, but my hands had not praised God that day. Suddenly at the end of the day I was expecting them to do so? That moment of inconsistency kept popping into my head when I started working on this song.

The lyrics began in my car. I was having a little worship time and remembered my empty hands at the Third Day concert. It was a big moment for me when I heard the first line come out of my mouth. I thought, *"Whoa, that's it right there."*

Months before we were scheduled to record our second album, I called the folks at our label and told them I had a definite idea for the direction of the CD. It was *Lifesong.* I knew the entire CD would revolve around this central theme, so I thought it should be the title track. "This is the name of the record," I said, because everything else is simply an overflow—evangelism, ministry, service, and fellowship. The whole spectrum emerges from my heart being right before God.

The label loved it. Mark Miller, our producer, loved it. That was it. In a couple of phone calls, the direction of the second album was set. There were no marketing meetings or haggling over what would sell and what would not sell. There was no pressure, not even a suggestion. They let the Lord lead me, and for that I am thankful.

I'm also thankful they always let me say what I think the Lord wants me to say. That is rare in today's world of high commerce.

And this song raises some hard issues.

For me to live my life on my terms all week long and then wander into a church on Sunday and read a bunch of words off of the screen and call that worship is to misunderstand worship.

Colossians 3:17 states: *"And whatever you do, in word or deed, do everything in the name of the Lord Jesus, giving thanks to God the Father through him."* That means being able to sign His name to the end of your day. That means all of life is worship. If we are so accustomed to thinking of worship as mere music, then we should realize the song starts when we awake in the morning. Romans

8:29 reveals that God is glorifying Himself by conforming us into the image of His Son. He's turning us into Jesus so that we can do as Jesus did while on earth: He honored His Father by obeying Him and always doing His will. So everything we do should be intended as worship of God.

I tell my students and concert audiences that worship is praying without asking for anything. It's just loving on God and living for an audience of One. But that prayer extends through every breathing moment. Worship cannot be confined to a sanctuary, auditorium, or arena. Worship is life. It means living so that everything we do makes Jesus smile. Think about that for a moment.

Think about seeing Jesus smile....

Now think about your life being the reason He's smiling....

Is there any greater motivation?

I want to please God with everything I do; I want to honor Him with every aspect of my life. I cannot compartmentalize and reserve certain areas for myself, my family, my career, and my hobbies. No, I am entirely His. I am not my own; I was bought at a price, the highest one ever paid. (1 Corinthians 6:19-20) The overarching theme of God's Word is that He created us for a purpose—to honor and glorify Him—and He is so devoted to our fulfilling that purpose that He went to the greatest of lengths to facilitate it through the death and Resurrection of His Son.

How can we not live in full surrender? How can we not follow Paul, James, Jude and others and render ourselves "bondservants,"—willing slaves—to Jesus Christ? How can we not let our lifesongs sing to Him?

Vocation has nothing to do with it. Wealth and privilege have nothing to do with it. While my purpose is to bring Him glory and to be conformed to the image of His Son, along my journey I became a youth pastor. God had a ministry for me. He had spiritual gifts and talents reserved for me. He orchestrated *everything* for me to become a youth pastor.

He arranged your situation differently. He didn't equip everyone for full-time church ministry. He may have equipped you to become a doctor, a coach, a construction worker, or a mother, but the ultimate goal for all of us is the same. We are to bring God glory and to make Him smile in everything we do and to point others to Him. He's going to enable this by turning us into His Son from the inside out.

Therefore, my purpose in life is not to be a youth pastor. That's just a means to the end. My purpose in life is to bring God glory through everything I do. I get to be a youth pastor while I do it. I haven't always known that. I've had a lot of other goals, and I had to be the best at one pursuit or another. I had to go *do* all these things. I had purpose about doing those things, but now I'm starting to understand that my purpose is just to bring glory to God and to steer people to Him. My purpose has more to do with *being* than *doing*, because being who we should be always brings about doing what we should do.

Being God's servant means a life evident of submission. It is reflected in how I think, act, and speak—how I treat people and love those around me.

Lifesong was the first song we recorded for the second CD. Our label listened to it and said, "Well, there's your first single." That was good to hear because they hadn't heard any other songs yet. It was also good to hear because *Lifesong* itself had taken a radical turn from its original sound. The music in the chorus was more ballad-like in the first version.

Fittingly, the song evolved to its final arrangement in the same place it began—at an outdoor concert.

It was the summer of 2004, and I think it was only one year after I had attended the Third Day concert as nothing more than a youth pastor. Our first album was doing well, and we were headlining an outdoor festival for the first time. I had recently written *Lifesong*. The huge venue was packed.

Right in the middle of worship time, while hearing the crowd sing our songs and watching how they worshipped, *Lifesong* was bouncing around in my head. That's typical when I'm writing a new song. Even when I'm not consciously thinking about it, the song still churns around in my brain. All I could think of from the stage was, "I want to share with them the message of *Lifesong*."

While talking about the definition of worship, this song kept coming to the forefront of my mind. I guess the context of where I was and what I was hearing in my head brought me to a realization: This song needs to be more of an anthem than it does a prayerful, contemplative song. The verses are really thought-provoking and get in your head a little bit to ask the hard questions, but the chorus is more of a declaration.

As I thought about it, I could just hear that robust crowd singing the *Lifesong* chorus.

In the middle of the concert I realized the music needed to change from soft to ascendant. It needed to raise people's awareness of true worship. It needed to raise their idea of holy living. It needed to raise their spirits.

It needed to raise their holy hands.

THE GODLINE

The words popped into my head while I was driving, but they came from my remembrance of how I felt when looking at my unclean hands lifted to the risen Savior while at the Third Day concert.

> *Empty hands held high, such small sacrifice;*
> *If not joined with my life, I sing in vain tonight.*
> *May the words I say, and the things I do*
> *Make my lifesong sing, bring a smile to You.*

God reminded me that there must be more to worship than singing someone else's song. I can stand in a worship service and parrot the lyrics on the screen with the rest of the congregation, but I didn't write that song. I'm singing someone else's song, someone else's experience with God that they set to music. Just because I know it and can sing it while raising my hands does not make it worship. My heart makes it worship. My intentions make it worship. Everything about me makes it worship.

So I have to stand before my pierced Savior every time and ask myself some questions: How did I worship Him with my life this week? Today?

What has my lifesong *really* said?

THE BOTTOM LINE

- How is your worship life? Is your worship on Sunday mornings a reflection of a week spent in worship and obedience to the Lord? Or is your worship often muted because of a week spent living more for yourself than for Jesus?

- Can you honestly say that everything you do in word and deed is for the glory of the Lord? Do you consciously try to produce holiness, or are you so living for God that He simply spills out of you?

- When was the last time you came to the end of a day and realized that you could not "sign" God's name to it because your motives and actions did not honor Him? How did you feel? What was your response? Do such days encourage you to seek the Lord more fervently, or do they leave you feeling defeated and hopeless? Do you know enough of God's promises to respond in a God-honoring way?

CASTINGCROWNS.TV

VIDEO CLIP - "Lifesong" from the *Lifesong Live* DVD
You've read it! Now go watch & listen to these stories at
www.castingcrowns.tv

In his first full-time ministry position, Mark (rear) and youth ministry workers (left to right) Chris Russell, Eric Green, Ryan Garrett, and Jonathan Long formed a band called The New Life Rookies. This band debuted *Here I Go Again.*

Mark (left) formed Casting Crowns at Daytona First Baptist Church along with original band members (left to right) Brittany Kiel, Tanner Hendley, Hector Cervantes, Robbie Cervantes, Melodee DeVevo, and Juan DeVevo.

Mark and some of his students enjoy "Alien Night" at Eagle's Landing First Baptist Church. The theme was drawn from Ephesians 2:19: "So then you are no longer strangers and aliens, but you are fellow citizens with the saints and members of the household of God..."

Casting Crowns band members Mark Hall and Chris Huffman (center) and Hecto Cervantes (left) clown around with some of their students during "Eighties Nite" at Eagle Landing First Baptist Church.

Scott Devlin and Jessica Wolfe celebrate her 20th birthday two days before her fatal car accident as Scott followed her home at night.

Mark (second from right) poses with (left to right) Reagan Farris, Juan DeVevo, and Darren Hughes in the wilderness outside Jerusalem, Israel on a youth mission trip in summer 2005. Reagan serves as co-youth pastor with Mark at Eagle's Landing First Baptist Church, Juan is a guitarist with Casting Crowns, and Darren is the production manager for Casting Crowns.

Erin Browning at her last dance recital on May 15, 2004 at The Carolina Theatre in Greensboro, North Carolina. She joined her mother, Laurie, and sisters Caroline and Mary Beth for a dance performed to *Here I Go Again*. Laurie labels this photo simply, "Erin's Smile."

Mark and his wife Melanie arrive at the Grammy Awards in 2006. Casting Crowns won the Grammy for Best Pop/Contemporary Gospel Album for *Lifesong*.

At 16 years old, Lucci Brisc stood on God's Word, simple faith, and principle to help spark a revolution that overthrew Communism in Romania. Now 32 years old, Lucci works with fledgling Christian musicians and serves as music director at Glory to Him Fellowship Church in Ozark, Alabama.

Mark speaks to a familiar audience on one of the band's most exciting nights ever-the launch concert for Casting Crowns' debut album. The band chose to launch the album with a concert at their home church, Eagle's Landing First Baptist Church in McDonough, Georgia.

Darrell Jenkins hugs new friend Diana Lleshi during a mission trip to a children's orphanage in Saranda, Albania in December, 2005.

Mark Hall poses backstage with 2005 National League Most Valuable Player Albert Pujols of the St. Louis Cardinals. Albert, a huge Casting Crowns fan, autographed dozens of memorabilia items for the band, including a prized authentic jersey.

Mark enjoys one of his favorite pursuits—hanging out with students—while leading a youth conference at Timothy Christian School in Piscataway, New Jersey.

From left to right: Melodee and Juan DeVevo, Mark Hall, and Casting Crowns production manager Darren Hughes pose against the backdrop of Jerusalem during a youth mission trip in summer 2005.

Band members Andy Williams, Chris Huffman, Hector Cervantes, Megan Garrett, Mark Hall, Melodee DeVevo, and Juan DeVevo are all smiles after winning a Dove Award.

Mark performs at the piano during the *Lifesong* tour in 2005.

Praise You in This Storm

Trust in the LORD with all your heart,
and do not lean on your own understanding.
In all your ways acknowledge him,
and he will make straight your paths.
PROVERBS 3:5-6

HE GIVES,
AND TAKES AWAY

Laurie Edwards watched her little girl gasping for air and wanted to breathe for her. She wanted the Maker of breaths to swoop in and fill her child's lungs and dissolve every tumor with His mere glance. She wanted to hit the rewind button and travel back to June 2001 and start all over. She wanted another miracle.

It was in the early morning hours of Saturday, October 30, 2004. Ten-year-old Erin Browning lay in a hospice bed in her home, in such pain and shortness of breath that, in fear and exasperation, she could manage only one request of her mother.

"Just read the Scriptures!" she said.

So Laurie began reading the Scriptures. She included Erin's favorite passage, Proverbs 3:5-6. From 1 a.m. until 5 a.m., loved ones took turns reading aloud the Word of God over a child in the last, cruelest stages of cancer's grip. Little Erin had battled for more than three years. She was diagnosed with Ewing's Sarcoma, a particularly aggressive bone cancer, on September 11,

2001, of all days. While the world watched the smoke and rubble of New York's twin towers, a woman in Winston-Salem, North Carolina heard a doctor say her seven-year-old daughter was riddled with cancer, starting from the second toe of her left foot and running through her hip, lungs, shoulder, and skull.

And now the end was near. Laurie did her best to refuse to believe it. Her trust in the Lord remained steadfast. She was frightened and faithful all at once. She prayed for an eleventh-hour miracle.

So they did as Erin asked. They read the Scriptures.

Jeremiah 29:11
Matthew 17:20
Mark 9:23
Mark 11:24
John 15:5-7
Philippians 4:13
Philippians 4:19
James 1:23
1 Peter 5:10

Over and over, they read God's Word. At one point, Laurie placed her Bible on the floor and stood on it. She grabbed sheets of Scripture printed from her computer, and literally stood on the Word of God as she read over her child. Finally, after the long night of reading Scripture followed by another long night of hopeful prayer, Laurie consented for a hospice nurse to administer an IV with medicine that essentially placed Erin in a painless coma on Sunday afternoon. There would be no more gasping for breath, no more strain on the child. Laurie had delayed the IV as long as she could bear. She was afraid to think what it could mean.

"She told us that she loved us so much," Laurie said. "And we told her that we loved her so much...."

M

E-mail: Tuesday, June 15, 2004; 1:09 PM

Dear Prayer Warriors:

After Erin's back and neck pain reached a level of "20!" on a scale of
1 to 10 and her sleep was interrupted due to difficulty breathing while
lying down, I reluctantly agreed to have Hospice come and bring a
hospital bed for Erin. I thought I could fool Erin by calling it an
"adjustable" bed, but as soon as she saw it she knew what it was
and was quite upset. We had our first visit with Hospice this past
Friday and, although it was a very pleasant visit, many tears were
shed over the weekend. …Please pray that Erin will feel comfortable in
her new bed. She is by no means bed-ridden and is enjoying her lazy
summer. She seems to have the most fun when she gets a chance to
go swimming.
Laurie Edwards

I met Erin Browning on Valentine's Day, 2004 at Westover Church in
Greensboro, North Carolina. Laurie had visited our website to share Erin's
story. Erin loved Casting Crowns, and, after six years of dance lessons, had
choreographed a dance to our song *Here I Go Again*. When Laurie initially
contacted us, we made arrangements to meet Erin, Laurie, and the family
before our concert in Greensboro. Three months later, Erin danced for the last
time as her mother and two sisters joined her for a performance of *Here I Go
Again* at The Carolina Theatre.

I was gripped by the imagery of Laurie's standing on her Bible and
quoting Scripture over her sick little girl. After all the e-mail updates and

prayers, that moment melted my heart and sparked the lyrics to this song.

The band was touring and preparing for our second album, and I was busy with our youth ministry. I kept up with Erin's condition through Laurie's e-mails detailing the family's wrenching ordeal. Every e-mail described a change in Erin's condition. One e-mail would offer hope: "There is a new treatment we're going to try, so please be praying." So we'd pray, and then the next e-mail would report, "It's not working."

Sometimes Laurie would be sad. Other messages were funny. Sometimes she had questions: "What's going on? I feel like I'm all alone in this." But I noticed through the course of her communications that her worship never changed. Her love of Jesus remained fervent even though she questioned what was going on and didn't really understand the reasons. It was raw, rare faith, and it was inspiring.

On June 21, 2004, I e-mailed Laurie to tell her that I was writing a song for Erin entitled *Praise You in This Storm*. Upon the news, Erin screamed so loud that it hurt Laurie's ears. Erin never got to hear the song, but Laurie heard it for the first time when her mother bought the CD on the day it was released and took it to the school where Laurie works. The two women sat in the car, listened to the song, and "cried and cried and cried," Laurie said.

"Erin would be so happy to know that other people were being touched by something written for her, because she was never about herself. She was about other people," Laurie said. "Other kids at school would say 'I want to be like Erin.' And she would say, 'No, you don't. You want to be like Jesus.'"

I was impressed with Laurie's faith, but Laurie will tell you how much she was impressed with Erin's faith. Erin was six years old when she prayed to receive Christ after listening to the words of a song by Point of Grace. She was diagnosed with cancer when she was seven, and by the time she was eight she was visiting area churches to give her testimony, as Laurie describes below:

E-mail: Friday, July 9, 2004; 10:20 PM

Dear Prayer Warriors:

It started on Sunday, probably not unlike many Sundays that you have, too. We were running late for church, no one was getting along, and Erin started feeling bad shortly after getting to church. God sent five people to take care of Erin in the ladies bathroom. Some were massaging her back and tickling her arms and legs, one had some Bio-Freeze to put on her back, one went to the store to buy her some blue Gatorade, we were all praying for her, and one kept an eye on the time to let Erin know when it was her time to share. After all that, Erin felt well enough to share her sweet testimony with the congregation at Adams Farm Church ... and she did it with a SMILE!

Laurie Edwards

The first thing you noticed about Erin was her smile. It always arrived before she did. She maintained her wit throughout her ordeal, regularly making her heartsick parents laugh. On the day that she was scheduled for a chest X-ray that ultimately would reveal six cancerous tumors in her chest cavity, Erin walked into her parents' room to tell them how concerned she was about undergoing the X-ray.

"If I get skin cancer, I'm going to really be ticked," she quipped.

Another time, Erin's step-father, Joey, and two sisters were playing basketball in the driveway. Erin asked her mom to help her carry her oxygen tank down the front steps. She rolled her tank onto the driveway, stopped the action, and said, "OK, whose team am I on?"

Erin always had been an active child. In fact, she learned she had cancer only after injuring herself while roughhousing on the sofa. She lay down to churn her feet in the air but kicked the top of her left foot. There was a loud pop that even Laurie heard. Erin cried, which was unusual for her. When the swelling never subsided, she eventually went for an MRI that revealed a tumor. The family still wasn't alarmed, thinking the mass only a part of the original injury.

Erin traveled to Baptist Hospital in Winston-Salem for a needle biopsy, which revealed the Ewing's Sarcoma. Next came the fateful bone scan and its overwhelming news on September 11.

Then God intervened.

Four prayerful months after the first bone scan, Erin underwent a second scan. This time, the cancer was gone. Doctors called the results remarkable. Laurie and Erin called it a miracle. That was all Erin needed to hear. Emboldened by the Lord's clear hand in her life, she began regularly sharing her faith and giving her testimony.

"She had a desire to reach people to let them know there is no hope or joy without God. And even though she had reason in her life not to be happy, she was joyful because she had Jesus in her heart," Laurie said. "She wasn't afraid. She let the Lord speak through her, and when she would get up and speak it was like I wasn't listening to my own daughter. He would put words in her mouth, and it was just awesome."

In September 2003, two years after her original diagnosis and 20 months after the second bone scan revealed no cancer, Erin underwent a checkup. Tests revealed a spot on her lung. It was surgically removed. Another checkup in December revealed no further spots. I met Erin for the first time in February. One month later, in March of 2004, another test showed the cancer had returned. There were six tumors in and around her lungs and chest cavity.

This time, the cancer didn't go away.

The tumors grew so large that they displaced organs and created a visible bulge in Erin's chest. They pressed down on her spleen, pushed her heart to the right, and deviated her trachea, straining her breathing.

E-mail: Friday, July 2, 2004; 9:23 AM

Dear Prayer Warriors:

The doctor said Erin is a phenomenal patient and he wished all his patients could be like her. He said he has never had a Ewing's Sarcoma patient with cancer in every bone he knew a name for who has done as well as Erin! He continued to praise Erin by commenting on how she positively touches everyone with whom she comes in contact. She makes you think about what is really important in life.

Although the doctor does not think Erin has much longer, he agreed that we should not give up hope…and we WILL NOT! He said you never know what God is going to do.

Laurie Edwards

Erin stayed as active as possible during her last summer. Her pain level subsided in late July, and in August she started fifth grade at High Point Christian Academy after finishing fourth grade with all A's.

In late August, Erin was hospitalized with severe chest pain and difficulty breathing. Her health began to deteriorate, and by the end of October Laurie's e-mail updates were desperate. Her last one before Erin's death came on October 30 and was a simple request in all caps: "PLEASE PRAY FOR ERIN!" It was the night in which Laurie stood on her Bible during the four hours of Scripture reading. The weekend crept into Saturday, when at 1:15 a.m. the hospice nurse told Laurie that Erin's vital signs and statistics suggested she had only approximately 20 minutes to live.

Fifty-one hours later, Erin finally gave up her fight.

In the early morning hours of Monday, Joey placed Laurie's sleeping bag on the floor beside Erin's bed. Laurie had not slept for 24 hours and was exhausted but wanted to stay with her unconscious daughter. At 1 a.m., Laurie lay down for a nap but prayed, "Lord, please wake me if Erin should need me."

Two hours later, Laurie awoke. Erin had not moved. As Laurie began praying, Erin lifted her head.

"Erin, do you want to sit up?" asked Laurie, who beckoned Joey at 3 a.m. to help her lift Erin into her arms. Laurie sat at the head of the bed and held Erin, who remained unconscious. Erin loved to hear Laurie's childhood stories, especially those describing how Laurie got into trouble for one minor trespass or another. So Laurie told Erin her stories again. She tickled Erin's face. She played with her hair. She whispered a mother's whisper.

At 4:10 a.m., Erin's breathing slowed. Laurie called in the rest of the family, and everyone stayed until Erin's last breath. Fourteen minutes later, Erin suddenly opened her eyes. Laurie said her first thought was not, *"Oh, she's waking up!"* It was a different kind of look. Laurie spoke to her daughter one last time.

"Oh, Erin, do you see Jesus?" Laurie asked. The nurses had warned Laurie that at the end Erin would gasp or grunt as she struggled for breath. She didn't.

"Erin, I think the angels have come to take you home," Laurie said. "You go see Jesus, and I'll see you soon."

Erin Browning went home at 4:24 a.m. on November 1, 2004.

Laurie still doesn't fully understand what happened next. She remembers only a tremendous peace and describes it as being under the shower of the Holy Spirit. She held Erin's body for 90 minutes while her daughter played in heaven.

"It was not like how I expected her last minutes to be. I thought I'd be hysterical, but I wasn't," Laurie said. "But she was where she always wanted to be. She told me when she was six years old that she couldn't wait to get to heaven. She said she had felt an emptiness in her heart, but when she asked

Jesus into her heart she never felt it again because Jesus had filled her and would never leave her. For the 10 years she was on this earth, God used her in a remarkable, powerful way.

"I've learned that He can use an average, ordinary family to do extraordinary things and that He continues to use us despite ourselves. We are so far from perfect, but He continues to use us," Laurie said. "I don't feel very strong, but apparently I appear strong outwardly, and God has used that to help others going through cancer and divorce to find a peace. How He has done that is beyond me. But He has a plan and purpose. A lot of times I may not like His plan, but I accept it. I'm just honored that He chose to use Erin and this family as He has."

Through it all, I was captured not just by Laurie's faith but also by her worship. She had the worship of Job:

> *The LORD gave, and the LORD has taken away; blessed be the name of the LORD.*
>
> *Job 1:21*

I have a son and two daughters, and I was amazed at how Laurie faced a parent's greatest fear. It doesn't mean that she wasn't angry. It doesn't mean that she wasn't sad or doubtful, but at the base of it she was leaning on God even if she was angry, sad, or doubtful. I was reminded once again that just because we cannot see God's purpose does not mean He doesn't have one. I was reminded that God is faithful, regardless of the circumstances. I was reminded that God is sovereign, and we're not.

Finally, I was reminded that we cannot control how long our lifesongs last. We only can control how loud we sing them. Little Erin lived out loud for Jesus. Even her e-mails were in all caps.

I heard from her for the final time in August, just over two months before she died. She danced until the very end.

E-mail: Sunday, August 22, 2004; 6:29 PM

HI MARK,

I WAS JUST WONDERING HOW THE NEW SONG IS GOING (*PRAISE YOU IN THIS STORM*). HAVE YOU BEEN WRITING A LOT OF NEW SONGS OR ARE YOU STAYING TOO BUSY TO? I CAN'T WAIT TO HEAR YOUR NEXT CD! I HAVE SIGNED UP TO TAKE LITURGICAL DANCE THIS YEAR EVEN THOUGH MOM DIDN'T THINK I SHOULD. I TOLD HER IF WE ARE PRAYING FOR A MIRACLE AND EXPECTING ONE, THEN WHY SHOULDN'T I TAKE DANCE? SO SHE LET ME!

PLEASE TELL THE BAND "HELLO" FROM ME! I PRAY THAT GOD WILL BLESS YOU JUST LIKE HE HAS ME.

LOVE,
ERIN

THE GODLINE

Were I to designate a Godline for this song, I would have to write every lyric. The whole song is a Godline. When it comes to writing, I wasn't there for this one. I can't think of anything for which I should ever take credit.

There are so many lines that gripped me as this came together. The first one was:

For You are who You are, no matter where I am.

I'm saying, "You're not God based on my circumstances." That was a big line when I sang it aloud for the first time. The first line that came to me concerning Erin's battle with cancer was the first verse:

I was sure by now, God, You would have reached down,
And wiped our tears away, stepped in and saved the day.
But once again, I say "Amen," and it's still raining.

It took me a while to be able to sing that verse aloud. I was too emotional over Erin and Laurie. The bridge also is special to me. In remembering Laurie's update about reading Scripture verses over Erin, I added Psalm 121:1-2 as the bridge to try to capture the cry of a desperate mother. That's why I repeat the lines with increasing fervor:

I lift my eyes unto the hills; where does my help come from?
My help comes from the Lord, the Maker of heaven and earth.

Last summer, we took several of our student leaders on a mission trip to Israel, where we traveled to the very area where it is believed Psalm 121 was possibly written. Our guide showed us all of the surrounding mountains and hills and said the armies of Israel's enemies built altars to pagan gods on every hill. Everywhere the Israelites looked, they saw pagan gods. They saw lies all around them. In that context, the verses take on an interesting slant: "I lift my eyes unto the hills. Where does my help come from? My help comes from the Lord."

Sometimes we all feel that way, don't we? What wonderful assurance that verse provides.

I can remember exiting the interstate while returning home from Nashville when the second verse came to me:

I remember when...I stumbled in the wind;
You heard my cry to You, and raised me up again.
My strength is almost gone; how can I carry on,
If I can't find You?

I'm saying, "God, I remember when this happened before and You pulled me out of it. But right now, my strength is almost gone and I don't know how I'm going to make it through this when I feel so alone and can't seem to find You." I'm sure we've all felt those emotions to some degree.

What is so remarkable about this song—and the very reason that I believe the entire song is a Godline—is how God already has used it. His reach extends beyond just those struggling with long-term or terminal illness. Somehow, God's providence made this song also apply to Hurricane Katrina.

Look back at the italicized verses above and consider them in light of the hurricane and its aftermath. Do the lyrics not fit the circumstances perfectly? Obviously, that wasn't me. That was the Lord. Now read the channel:

As the thunder rolls, I barely hear You whisper through the rain,
"I'm with you."
And as Your mercy falls, I raise my hands and praise the God who gives,
And takes away.

Amazing, huh? Now consider that this album was released on Tuesday, August 30, the day after Katrina devastated New Orleans and much of the Gulf Coast. By the end of the week, a disc jockey somewhere produced a new mix for *Praise You in This Storm*. He spliced into the song sound bytes of news reports and even President George W. Bush speaking, and the result registered high on the goosebump meter.

While I wrote the song from my exposure to one family's battle with cancer, I realized it would apply to many people who are dealing with tragedy and heartbreak. We've all been there, so I figured it would touch a nerve. But how could I have known it would have anything to do with a national disaster?

We finally heard the disc jockey's mix while in the car. As I sat there, it was like God gave a whole new meaning to a song I had written—as if it were written for that too. Everything fits, the words in the song perfectly complementing the news excerpts. The quotes are spliced so that the questions are right next to the answers in the song. One of the excerpts has a hurricane victim asking aloud, "What are we going to do? Where are we going to go?" It is immediately followed by the bridge: "I lift my eyes unto the hills/Where does my help come from?/My help comes from the Lord/The Maker of heaven and earth."

I sat in my car and stared. "Unbelievable," I muttered. You think you know what God is up to, and then He takes a song you wrote four or five months before and unveils an entirely new purpose for it.

Behold, He indeed makes all things new. That's what He did for this song. And that's what He did for little Erin.

THE BOTTOM LINE

- Do you view trials in your life as God's abandonment of you—or as opportunities for you to abandon yourself to God? Explain your answer.

- What is your favorite Biblical example of someone persevering through a trial? Why? What part of the story most inspires you? What lessons have you taken from that account and attempted to apply to your life?

- In Job 1, the beleaguered Job professes that the Lord gave him everything he ever had and also reserved the right to take away everything. Earlier in the chapter, God gave Satan permission to test Job—and it was God who began the discourse on Job in the first place. What does this say about God's sovereignty? His justice? What does your response say about your level of trust?

CASTINGCROWNS.TV

VIDEO CLIP - "Praise You In This Storm" from the *Lifesong Live* DVD You've read it! Now go watch & listen to these stories at www.castingcrowns.tv

Does Anybody Hear Her?

"Come to me, all who labor and are heavy laden,
and I will give you rest. Take my yoke upon you,
and learn from me, for I am gentle and lowly in heart,
and you will find rest for your souls.
For my yoke is easy, and my burden is light."
MATTHEW 11:28-30

THREE MORE STEPS BEHIND

I n 2004, former National Football League lineman Ed Tandy McGlasson, now a pastor in Anaheim, California, published his first book. It was entitled *The Difference a Father Makes*, and it details his interesting approach to transforming his boys and girls into godly men and women.

McGlasson devotes much of his book to discussing the rituals he has developed with each of his five children, but his unique rite of passage for his daughters was most touching. When his daughters reached 14 years of age, McGlasson chose to let each know that she had reached womanhood. His method was ingenious and powerful—an approach that gave them an identity and assurances they will remember for the rest of their lives.

In the case of his oldest daughter, Jessica, McGlasson asked her for a date, took her to a nice local restaurant, and bought her the meal of her choice.

Then McGlasson proclaimed the importance of the day—and helped set the course of Jessica's life—by telling her that she is now a woman. He expected her to act accordingly. He smiled and cried as he told her how beautiful she is and how special she is to the family and to him. He affirmed her by lovingly telling her all about her wonderful attributes. Then he stunned the restaurant's patrons.

This huge, burly former New York Giants lineman pulled a promise ring out of a flower and got down on one knee.

"'Jessica, I am giving you this ring today. Are you willing to make a covenant before the Lord tonight, that on your wedding night you will be prepared to present this ring to your husband and say to him, "This ring represents a covenant I made with my dad, that I would save myself until I got married. And I have done so"? Will you wear this ring?'"[1]

Jessica wept. Her daddy wept. McGlasson slipped a promise ring on her finger to highlight Jessica's rite of passage into womanhood.

On separate occasions, each of McGlasson's daughters promised to reserve herself for the husband God has for her and to honor the Lord with her choices. Looking back, McGlasson has witnessed remarkable growth in his daughters since their individual rites of passage.

Why? What triggered the girls' maturity and integrity amid a difficult teenage culture? Could it have been their parents' total involvement in their lives? Was it because they didn't have to wonder how their parents felt about them? Do you think those young ladies feel wanted? Needed? Affirmed?

Do you think they know that their daddy loves them?

M

I'm not sure how the woman at the well (John 4) would have reacted had she heard *Does Anybody Hear Her?* But I do know how teenage girls in my student ministry have reacted. By the looks on their faces after they hear it, the apparent answer to the question posed by the song is a resounding, *"No, no one is listening."*

I still call it "The Girl Song." Most of the time, I sing a song repeatedly in my head until I record it, and then I stop. I haven't stopped singing "The Girl Song" yet.

The *Lifesong* album was finished but was yet to be released in the summer of 2005 when I saw a preview of how this song hits a nerve. We were taking a group of our students to a barbecue restaurant when three of the girls asked to hear a few of the new songs. I had a copy of the master in my car, so they climbed in as I turned up the volume before becoming engrossed in a telephone call. They listened to *Lifesong* first and were grooving to it, smiling, and trying to remember the words.

I was still distracted on the phone moments later when I realized that the van was ready to leave for the restaurant, and the rest of the group was waiting on the girls and me to hop aboard. I was trying to end the phone conversation and usher the girls out of the car when I realized "The Girl Song" was playing. I paused, hung up the phone and glanced at the girls. All three had their heads down and were looking at their laps. One of them was sniffing.

By the first chorus.

It was almost as if the subject of the song was sitting in my car. That's when I knew, *Yeah, it speaks to them.* And it wasn't really surprising, because the song depicts where so many of them live.

Adults live there, too, if we're being honest. We crave approval regardless of age. We adults separate ourselves from teenagers, thinking they are so different. The only differences of note are the level of influence and responsibilities. But we're still basically like we were as teenagers: We want to be accepted; we want to be treated well; we want to be respected and even liked. When we're not, it hurts. When we're left out, it hurts. When we're bullied, it hurts. We all feel the same emotions. So teenagers aren't aliens or robots. They're just younger, more immature versions of us.

I needed almost a decade to write this song. You may recall that it is something of an offshoot of one of the songs on our first CD. I realized that the meaty second verse of *What If His People Prayed?* was really its own song—that one simple paragraph was an injustice to the girl I was seeing far too frequently in far too many places. I had to let the story play out in my head for a while. Unfortunately, as a youth pastor I've had more case studies than I have ever wanted.

During my first few years of student ministry I began seeing something in teenage girls that I'd never noticed before. Consistently, I saw that each had an internal, overwhelming need for her daddy's love.

In my formative years as a youth pastor, I learned a great deal about student ministry from Roger Glidewell, a mentor with Global Youth Ministries. His principal lesson was that a teenage girl's foremost desire is *approval* from her father. She wants to know that she has normal needs and emotions and that she is wanted and needed and approved.

If she can't get dad's approval, she will take a step down: She will find somebody—anybody—who will at least accept her. Maybe the person doesn't especially like the teenage girl, but he or she will let her hang around. So a teenage girl will settle for *acceptance.*

If she can't get dad's approval or acceptance, she will get his *attention.* She's going to get dad to notice her one way or another. She will steadily lower the bar until she finds whatever is closest to what she thinks she needs.

I've seen it so often that now it has become the norm.

We have before us a lost generation of teenage girls, essentially orphaned under their own roofs by parents with better things to do and more important people to see. The girl in the song is a result of this scenario, one that I see played out with alarming consistency even within the Church.

So many girls tell me, in various ways, that all they want is for their parents, and especially dad, to approve of them. But he doesn't, or at least he doesn't demonstrate it, so they go looking for the next best thing—just anybody who will love them and offer a measure of intimacy for which they so desperately long. I've seen girls totally give themselves away just to have someone "love" them. Those girls have phoned me or sat in my office and wept, the mistakes and the pain coming in waves.

My first three years in full-time student ministry were at Center Hill Baptist Church, where the first line of the song surfaced as I began noticing the culture of these girls.

She is running…a hundred miles an hour…in the wrong direction.

Why could I see it when the girls could not see it? Even worse: Why could I see it so well while some parents were so blind? Many parents have proven in conversations and conduct that they simply don't grasp the pervasiveness of this problem.

But parents also don't have much help. One of my greatest ministry obstacles is an MTV pop culture that makes no bones about going after the souls of our youth. Let me cite an example of what we face:

Many of these girls who settle for getting people's attention are on a quest to find something to "complete" them. They have the notion that it is possible for someone to complete them because that's what the movies and the Top 40 radio countdown assures them. Songs blare the promise that someone is "all I need." The dashing Tom Cruise looks into the eyes of the beautiful Renee Zellweger and pines, "You complete me." That's one of the scariest lines ever to come out of Hollywood. People were not created to complete people. It's impossible. In my opinion, that is why so many marriages fail.

People enter into relationships incomplete because they don't have a relationship with God or they have a very immature one. They expect a person to fill all of life's voids, but people weren't created to fill a void that only God can fill.

When we look for someone other than God to complete us, we remain needy, and neediness is poison to a relationship.

But the masses take the bait and launch into a never-ending, bar-hopping, bed-swapping quest to find the person who "completes" them—to provide the love that daddy never did and fill the void that only God can.

Girls are being told lies about who they are when, really, they're princesses. They're priceless, but they're being told by the world:

> *You're going to have to sell yourself. You have to present a certain look and act a certain way. These people over here expect you to hold this look and lifestyle a priority, but that group over there says you must do something different to get what you want. And if you can't pull it off and keep everyone happy, you don't belong. You'll be rejected, you won't be happy, and you'll be a nobody.*

Girls constantly have to sell themselves to everyone, or at least they're made to feel they must, and the ultimate fallout is usually painful. Their need for approval and for someone to tell them they are OK is sometimes worth more to them than their self-respect.

I made sure the song examined the *results* of such life choices. I wanted to show the aftermath. I wanted to check in on this girl after her decisions had fermented into a misspent youth and destructive adulthood.

The girl in the song becomes a young lady who eventually realizes that she's given too much of herself away and she's way out there now. In fact, she feels like she's almost too far gone, but there is no such territory with a God of unconditional love.

So the song is intended for two audiences.

It's a song to this girl, because I want her to see that God loves her just like she is. He knows everything that has happened, yet He is calling her out anyway. (Matthew 11:28-30; 2 Corinthians 5:20-21). She's another two years older and she's three more steps behind, but she's never out of the Lord's reach.

However, this song also is aimed at the Church. You see, this girl needs to know that God loves her and has a plan for her life…but *we* need to know that God loves her and has a plan for her life.

We believers tend to maintain at least two "bad" lists. I'm an expert at it. If someone does something on one bad list, we're willing to restore her, love on her, pray for her, circle around her, and escort her back into the fold. But what if she does something on the other bad list? Then everybody needs to just back away and try not to get anything on them.

I often remind myself: If I imagine the person with the worst reputation ever, I'm only two or three bad decisions away from being that person. Those of us who keep lists should examine our hearts, our pasts, and our habits. May Christ's love overwhelm all of our preconceived notions.

I have been frank in this chapter because of the dire spiritual condition of our youth. I sense it when I visit school campuses. There is an indescribable weight of heaviness when you walk through those doors, demanding that students prove themselves to somebody. Ninth grade seems to be the most crucial year. Students can reach somewhat of a level of security in their identities through eighth grade. Suddenly, they're nobodies again when entering high school. They face a decision as freshmen: *What am I willing to do to fit in? How far am I willing to go? Who is going to accept me? What group of people at lunch is going to let me sit with them?*

I've seen teenagers change everything about themselves just because a group let them hang out with them or someone accepted them. It doesn't always matter who offers the acceptance, just as long as it is offered.

The student often thinks that no one understands her or no one has ever gone through what she is feeling. Her friends certainly don't talk about it. Kids talk all the time without saying anything; they never really share their feelings with each other. Everyone is guarded.

It's a scary place to live if there is not a Rock in the kid's life.

Parents, church leaders, believers everywhere, will you join me in a commitment to invest the love of Christ in our young people like never before? This isn't something we need to "pray about." This is already within God's will. Will we suffer the children to come to Him?

I am not exaggerating when I insist that the Body of Christ is losing the war for the souls of the student body of America. In watching the Public Broadcasting Service's 1999 *Frontline* documentary *The Lost Children of Rockdale*

County, I heard one sordid story after another describing the carnal escapades of children participating in random and group sex (including homosexuality) that led to a syphilis outbreak. Some observers have intimated that the teen behavior detailed in the Frontline special is isolated.

Dr. Robert Blum disagrees. Dr. Blum is a professor and director of the division of general pediatrics and adolescent health at the University of Minnesota in Minneapolis. After watching *The Lost Children of Rockdale County*, Dr. Blum wrote a response for PBS.org in which he cited a disconnect between aimless, bewildered children and "parents who are either clueless or blatantly unconcerned about their children. We see parents who have replaced caring and personal involvement with the purchase of material goods and we see parents who are afraid to discipline their children."[2]

Dr. Blum then offered a conclusion that for years as a student pastor I have suspected is true.

"What is so disturbing about the program is not that we are witnessing a rare event in the United States, but rather an event that is quite common," Blum writes. "First of all, the use of sex to attract friendships and maintain social connections (or to disrupt others' social connections) is age old and the fact that this is a white upper income community does not make it particularly surprising despite the editorial comments of the commentator. Rather, there may be a perception (there appears to be this bias in the program) that these events are rare in suburban America. The events are not rare; it may be that as adults we tend to be less willing to acknowledge them in this kind of community than in lower income communities."[3]

How isolated is this teen behavior? Let me tell you just how close to home it can hit: I live within five miles of the Rockdale County line. That documentary was filmed in the neighboring county. And it just as easily could have been filmed in yours or mine.

On the documentary I saw one child after another crying out in their different ways, and I was left wondering: Are we listening? Do we care?

Does anybody hear them?

THE GODLINE

I repeat the bridge twice in this song for emphasis. It is the Godline and the line that packs the most punch:

If judgment looms under every steeple,
If lofty glances from lofty people,
Can't see past her scarlet letter…
And we've never even met her.

I often live by a stereotypical picture of what I will not accept and to whom I cannot attach myself because it would damage my witness—whatever that is in my mind. So there have been times when someone who looked like the person described in this song walked into church, and I quickly sized her up and backed off.

She's a lost cause. She's a bad influence.

Do you see the danger there? Suddenly, she went from being a person with hurts and needs to being only a bad influence with carry-on baggage. Failure is not a person. Failure is an event, but Satan tells this girl: "This is your life. This is how your life is always going to be. Nothing will ever be any different than it is right now." Yet God faithfully answers, "No, this is today. I'm trying to carry you into tomorrow. I can move you past this."

We should help her listen to the right voice. Unfortunately, we believers often communicate to her the same lie uttered by the enemy: *This is you. This is who you are.*

Sometimes those who are hurting can't hear God above the nasty clamor of His people.

THE BOTTOM LINE

- Can you name an instance in which you treated someone differently or saw someone treated differently because of his or her "bad name" or poor reputation? How did the person with the poor reputation respond?
- If you know someone has fallen morally or legally, how do you respond to him? Do you engage with him? How? Do you ignore him? How could you improve in your approach to such situations?
- In what ways has our culture influenced young people's decision-making? How can the Church respond?

CASTINGCROWNS.TV

VIDEO CLIP - "Does Anybody Hear Her" from the *Lifesong Live* DVD
You've read it! Now go watch & listen to these stories at
www.castingcrowns.tv

Stained Glass Masquerade

"Woe to you, scribes and Pharisees, hypocrites!
For you are like whitewashed tombs, which outwardly
appear beautiful, but within are full of dead people's
bones and all uncleanness. So you also outwardly
appear righteous to others, but within
you are full of hypocrisy and lawlessness."

MATTHEW 23:27-28

HAPPY PLASTIC PEOPLE

The haze that covered the south Alabama summer afternoon was a concoction of at least three obnoxious ingredients: humidity crawling in from the Gulf Coast, exhaust fumes puffing up from the highway in front of our home—and Love Bugs.

Millions and millions of tiny, black, swarming, incessantly pestering Love Bugs.

They're like gnats on steroids and apparently are attracted to car exhaust because they hovered in a black cloud on either side of the highway. Unfortunately, they're obviously immune to the carbon monoxide from the exhaust.

I sat in the swing on my wraparound front porch in Samson, Alabama. Through His sheer favor, God blessed us with a landlord who rented us his turn-of-the-century home—complete with hardwood floors and high ceilings—far below market value. It was great for entertaining when we invited over some of our students. I was a part-time student pastor, still learning the ministerial ropes while also attending college in the mornings.

As much as I learned in college, my greatest lessons in ministry always have come in the real world. And usually the hard way.

Two major events occurred in relatively short sequence, giving early shape to my ministry philosophy. The first was a student conference featuring Dave Edwards, whom you met in an earlier chapter. Dave was the first person I had ever heard publicly admit that he had dyslexia. Shortly afterward, I left New Zion Baptist in Bonifay, Florida and moved to Samson (Alabama) First Baptist.

That's where the second ministry-altering event occurred—in my swing on that wraparound porch as I swatted away at Love Bugs. I never saw it coming.

His name was Larry, and I've never forgotten him because of what he taught me. Only 15 years old, Larry wanted to talk. He was exasperated and needed some counsel. Almost sheepishly, he revealed that he had tried repeatedly to overcome a particular problem—I believe it was his temper—but had met with only frustration.

"Yeah, man, I know how that goes. I struggle with that, too," I said. "And I still mess up."

His head snapped around, his eyes wide open. "You mess up?" I was stunned at his reaction, but I tried to appear unfazed. His words hit hard.

I thought to myself, *"What have I been teaching during my first few months here—that I'm some sort of up-in-the-clouds guy who never makes any mistakes? Have I been teaching lessons instead of teaching students? Have I only regurgitated Biblical wisdom that I heard in school earlier in the day? Am I loving on these kids from below—or shooting down from above?"*

So I answered Larry even as my mind reeled.

"Yeah, dude, I still mess up," I said. "Man, I've blown it a hundred times today. Melanie said something to me and I spouted off at her, and then a guy pulled out in front of me this morning and I popped off at him."

I still remember the look on his face. It was a mix of relief and incredulous disbelief.

"Man, oh, man," he exhaled. "It feels good to know that someone else is dealing with this."

Once again, his words cut deep. I repeated his statement to myself: *"Somebody else is dealing with this? Good grief, we're just talking about temper. Does he think that nobody else in the Church has this problem?"*

It was an eye-opener to learn that someone struggling with such a common problem was so guarded because he felt no one would understand. But it was a real kick in the gut to discover I had fashioned such an image before my students that at least one of them thought he wasn't on my level.

Taken together, these teachable moments with Dave Edwards and Larry revealed that authentic Christianity is nothing if not transparent. Our Lord never put on airs. Why should we?

My conversation with Larry has affected how I engage in ministry to this day. Whether I'm onstage or in casual conversation, I speak to my students differently because of him. The experience even led to my unearthing another layer of truth in Scripture. In John 3:30, John the Baptist refers to Jesus and says, "He must increase, but I must decrease."

My conversation with Larry cast the verse in a different light: I must decrease before these kids so they will have a greater chance to increase. I must become humble, meek, transparent, and approachable. I must become real. I must never be an ivory-tower preacher. I must live a real life in a real world... just as they do.

Instead of building walls to hide my weaknesses—like those I had expertly crafted my entire life—I should expose my weaknesses. Even when it is humiliating. I have to decrease even in the students' respect of me, because they don't need a hero. They need the Savior. So if knowing Jesus means they have to discover that I don't have it all together—and if I'm a little less cool in their eyes—then so be it.

I make sure to convey this message in concerts today.

When we're onstage, my goal is to *prove* to you that God can use anybody. The Apostle Paul took the same approach: "I *boast* in my weakness" (2

Corinthians 12:9). He calls himself the foremost, or chief, of sinners. (1 Timothy 1:15) In Romans 7, he laments his inability to control himself, saying he does what he most wishes he would not do and fails to do what he most longs to do. He constantly points back to his old self, saying he had been blasphemous and insolent, or riotous. (1 Timothy 1:13) Anytime he felt people were putting too much emphasis on him, he instantly showed them the real Paul, warts and all.

Over time, I learned to follow his lead with my students—and with everyone in the Church.

I often talk about my shortcomings. Sometimes it has hurt me. Sometimes students and even co-laborers have joked about my absent-mindedness or ADD: "Well, you know Mark…he doesn't know anything, ha, ha, ha." I occasionally face those attitudes. So I pause and ask myself, "What's the point here? Is it to be respected and thought of as awesome, or is it for this person, after he's finished trashing me, to realize that God can use anybody?"

I personally may never see the person come to that realization, which can be frustrating. Our flesh wants to see immediate results when we put our heads on the chopping block. Personal gratification doesn't always come, however. Sometimes, we just have to trust that God is going to use it in some way, some day.

E-mail: Sunday, August 21, 2005; 9:11 PM

Dear Casting Crowns:

I've had the chance to hear two of the songs that are to be released on your new album, Lifesong. The lyrics…WOW. They both really hit my heart hard.

I recommitted my life to Christ two years ago and it's been a big struggle since that day. I was raised in a Christian home but turned from God when my father died when I was 17. Because of the things I did in the following years and the Christians that I knew, I understood completely the song *Does Anybody Hear Her?*. It hit very close to home because of the church I was raised in. When the youth group found out about my life and where it stood after my father's death, they pushed me out very slowly. But the push was enough to drive me away for many years to follow, because even after the anger of my father's death wore off, I honestly didn't want anything more to do with church because of my experience.

I recommitted my life to Christ at the age of 24, striving very hard to live a Christian life without a church. I didn't want to step foot into another church because of what had happened. Even when I started looking for a church a year later, I was afraid to open up to anyone about my past and the road I had walked. I was afraid that, if they learned the secrets my past held, then I would be pushed away from the church again—which meant I kept God at a distance without realizing it.

That is where your second song I heard starts to hit home. It is *Stained Glass Masquerade*. So many times over the last year I've found myself so close to just falling apart, but I walk in that church and wear that smile and put up the wall, hoping it appears that I'm just like everyone else.

I have found a church and have been there for a year now. I've started opening up in some ways, but in others I'm still very much holding back. In a sense I'm still putting up that mask and pretending everything is OK. Within the last several weeks, before hearing the song, I have been so close to breaking down. At the same time I've wondered whether it is normal to feel like this. Do others ever feel this way, or am I doing something wrong in my walk? I see others in my church and it seems like they have it all together. I sit there thinking, *"What's wrong with me?"*...The only thing I know for a fact is that, even though I'm only 26, I want to surrender so much more of my life to God. The question is: How do I get there from where I am currently in my walk? Right now, the answer might not be vividly clear, but that song has helped me realize that I shouldn't give up and to keep striving and seeking after Him because I'm not alone.

God bless and keep you,
Billi

I often tell my students that we are happy plastic people, so I finally wrote a song about it. *Stained Glass Masquerade* describes my own struggles with image manufacturing. It's called religion, and my Pharisaical robe has more tassels than most.

Growing up in a church that didn't talk about personal sins and struggles rendered me a young adult who didn't talk about sins and struggles. That's not good when you're becoming a minister.

I sketched a mental picture of a strong Christian, someone who truly walks with Jesus. I formed this picture from what I had read and heard, and at church I strived to be that person. If there was anything in my life that didn't fit the mental picture, I had to bury it. I guess subconsciously I thought that if my church folks believed I was OK, then maybe I really was.

Sound familiar?

I don't think I'm alone. Our insistence on maintaining an image is the reason most believers rarely confess bitterness, jealousy, addiction, lust, self-hate, greed, and anger at God over tragedy or suffering. We keep simmering—but simmering beneath the surface. If that is the case in our lives, then people at church don't really know us. They know the person we play when we're there. Therein lies the rub: If we're not our true selves while walking around the church, then who are we when worship starts? At what point does the performance stop and the real believer start?

It's spooky when you're in church and the pastor is expounding truths that describe you—and it would stun everybody else in the room to know that about you.

When tragedy strikes under these circumstances and we must rely on the Lord and fellow believers, the people around us don't really know us. Then the facades crash to the floor and reality hits. As we lie vulnerable, Satan slips in with his uncanny timing and taps us on the shoulder:

> *Is any of this real?*
> *You're obviously not real...*
> *Is anyone else?*
> *Is God?*

This scenario may seem far-fetched, but I've learned personally that image manufacturing as a believer affects everything else. It affects my heart, my mind, my worship, and my ministry. In fact, role-playing and ministry are oil and water. That's when we perform ministry to be seen by those around us. Jesus warns us in Matthew 6 that God is so much more concerned about our hearts than He is our sacrifice. He looks at our motives first.

It seems we're missing so much in the area of fellowship. If only we authentically knew each other, it would be so much easier to loosen up and accept and love each other.

The concept for this song had been bubbling in my head for years, the foundation poured out by Larry on my front porch. I never knuckled down and put it into words until last year, and even then I needed a little help.

I knew Nicole Nordeman as an awesome songwriter, and I thought a fresh slant could make the song unique. I especially wanted a woman's perspective because girls face so many self-image issues within the pressures of our culture. I thought it would be interesting to hear how Nicole would capture that struggle.

When I told her my idea and shared what I had already written, she jumped on it. "You're right there where my heart is on this subject," she said.

We co-wrote the song primarily through e-mails and phone conversations. Nicole contributed the second verse, which is extremely strong. The vocal performance of that verse by our Megan Garrett is equally brilliant. Nicole also helped me with the chorus, and I love her line that says exactly what's been on my heart all these years about us happy plastic people: "If the invitation's open/To every heart that has been broken..."

Maybe then we close the curtain...on our tiring, useless, artificial, self-centered, Spirit-sapping stained glass masquerade.

THE GODLINE

I remember saying to myself, "Wooooo!" when the second half of the first verse came out of my mouth for the first time:

So I tuck it all away,
Like everything is OK;
If I make them all believe it,
Maybe I'll believe it too.

That's how I describe what I've done before—create a role in which I become a "super believer," all the while shielding my secret sins and innermost pain and acting as if I'm OK when I'm not. It reminds me of an interesting word study: Did you know that the Greek word for *actor*—the people who went onstage in Bible times to perform behind different masks for different scenes—is the word translated in English as *hypocrite*? That helps explain the remainder of the verse:

So with a painted grin,
I play the part again;
So maybe they will see me
The way that I see them.

One Godline did not make this song, but I use it in concerts and when I talk to my students. It summarizes the song perfectly:

I don't think it bothers the world so much that we sin; I think it bothers the world that we act like we don't.

THE BOTTOM LINE

- How genuine a believer are you? Do you live in two different worlds— your workaday world and your Sunday morning world? Are you the same person in both places?
- How transparent a believer are you? Do you know fellow believers you can trust? Do they truly know what is going on in your life? When is the last time you shared your heart with someone you trust? How did you feel, and what was the outcome?
- Read John 8:1-11. Why did Jesus respond to the woman as He did? Why did He respond to the crowd as He did?

CASTINGCROWNS.TV

VIDEO CLIP - "Stained Glass Masquerade" from the *Lifesong Live* DVD
You've read it! Now go watch & listen to these stories at
www.castingcrowns.tv

Blessed be the God and Father of our Lord Jesus
Christ, the Father of mercies and God of all comfort,
who comforts us in all our affliction, so that we may be
able to comfort those who are in any affliction, with the
comfort with which we ourselves are comforted by God.
For as we share abundantly in Christ's sufferings, so
through Christ we share abundantly in comfort too.
If we are afflicted, it is for your comfort and salvation;
and if we are comforted, it is for your comfort,
which you experience when you patiently endure the
same sufferings that we suffer. Our hope for you is
unshaken, for we know that as you share in our
sufferings, you will also share in our comfort.

2 CORINTHIANS 1:3-7

WHAT GOES AROUND COMES AROUND

At 6-foot-5 and 240 pounds as a ninth-grader, Steven Gerald was the definition of wrath on a football field. A student in tiny Samson, Alabama, Steven was known for two things: His size, and his ability to use it to win football games.

My co-youth pastor, Reagan Farris, also remembers Steven for teaching him a lifelong biblical illustration.

Reagan was only 5-feet-9, 130 pounds when he attended ninth grade with Steven. Like every other high school boy, Reagan wanted to be considered cool, so despite his size he found it difficult to refuse the challenge when friends baited him to join the football team. He had speed and toughness, but neither mattered much when Steven Gerald was on the other side of the line.

Reagan was playing receiver one day at practice when the coach called for a reverse. The quarterback would turn and pitch the ball to the running back, who would sweep to the right and hand it to Reagan, who was streaking back across the field to the left. Steven, however, threw a wrench in his plans.

Playing linebacker, Steven smelled out the play and met Reagan behind the line of scrimmage, picked him up and slammed him to the turf. Reagan doesn't exactly remember, but he thinks he momentarily blacked out. When his wits and breath returned, Reagan jumped to his feet and played off the moment as only a testosterone-filled teenage boy can: "Let's do it again! Come on, guys, block for me! Let's go! Let's do it again!"

Steven shrugged. Fine by him.

The offense lined up again. Once again, no blocker wanted any part of Steven. They invented ways to get out of his way, and he jetted to the backfield unhindered. There was tiny Reagan, speeding right back into the human wall. Steven met him, wrapped his arms around him, picked him up, and....

Gently laid him on the ground.

Steven patted Reagan on the back. "There you go, buddy." At that moment, Reagan says, God taught him the meaning of mercy.

It wasn't the last time Steven was involved in a lesson Reagan still remembers.

I was Reagan's youth pastor at Samson First Baptist when he was in high school with Steven. During the middle of a school day, news spread throughout town that Steven's father had been electrocuted while welding on an old cotton gin. Out of nowhere, this big, strapping man was killed, and the event rattled the entire town in south Alabama.

At the time, I had a group of about five or six "Timothys," high school understudies whom I was discipling. I met with them on the day of the accident and asked, "How is Steven doing? Is he OK?"

No answer.

They all looked down at their shoes, so I knew no one had talked to him. I also knew why. They didn't know what to say. How do you explain away such a tragedy? *"It's OK. God still loves you. Come on to church. Let's go to a youth rally together."*

No, their friend's dad had died. It was so heavy to these guys and hit them so hard that it made no sense. They didn't understand why it happened, so even they were questioning why God would allow something so drastic in this kid's life. They were dealing with their own issues: *"Who's to say it's not going to happen to me?"*

In the middle of their own turmoil, they nevertheless were believers whose friend needed comforting.

"I don't know what to say to him," one of them said.

I had learned during a few such scenarios that there is really nothing to say. But there is something *to do.*

"Guys, you've just got to go love him," I said. "Don't think you have to have all the answers. You don't have to make some great spiritual pronouncement when you see him. You just have to be there for him and tell him you're sorry for what happened to his daddy and that you love him. And then you just hang out with him. You've just got to go love him like Jesus—love him like He would, and love him to Jesus."

That statement painted two pictures for them—and for all of us.

First, we should love lost and hurting people like Jesus. How does He love them? When He was on earth, Jesus loved people where they were. He didn't take them to some giant, faraway truth. He met them in their individual situations and gently shared truth with them there.

Secondly, we also have to love people *to* Him. Our role as believers is to *be* Jesus to people by serving as His hands and feet. They should see Jesus in us as we help usher them to God's throne.

On our first album, I addressed a common dilemma with the song *Here I Go Again*: I love Jesus. I love my friend. I want to show Jesus to my friend. I'm trained well beyond my obedience, so despite being ready to share and initially willing to go, I invariably stumble when the moment arrives.

Love Them Like Jesus is the answer to the dilemma presented in *Here I Go Again*. I didn't want to leave people with an incomplete picture, so *Love Them Like Jesus* says, "Here's what you ought to do," and I share a lesson I have learned the hard way.

Too often I have stood tongue-tied before friends facing a giant issue in their lives. I have experienced the great fear most believers feel in those situations. We don't know why God brought or allowed the difficult circumstances, and sometimes we're angry at God, too. Amidst all of our own torn emotions, we think, *"I've got to go to this person and somehow try to make sense of it all."* We usually think that somehow we must defend God and His actions or seeming inaction. We believe we have to give a certain verse or say something to make everything better, because we want everything to be better for our friends.

Those kinds of thoughts are the very source of our reluctance to move.

All of the self-induced burden to make everything better creates a fear that causes us to pull away from our hurting friends. We heap all the pressure on ourselves. This is true even in a friendship between believers because we always want to have a spiritual answer for everything. We want to have the bow tied at the end. We want the quick resolution and immediate assurance that everything is going to be just fine.

Guess what? Sometimes it's not just fine. Sometimes you don't understand what's going on, and you're not going to know for a while, if at all. *Love Them Like Jesus* realizes that truth.

The song says, "OK, I can't solve the problem, but God doesn't need to be defended here." Our best bet is not to go to them with all of the answers but just to go to them, period. Just love on them. Just be there. Cry with them. Pray with them. Love on them. That doesn't mean we shouldn't share Scripture or give biblical encouragement. Obviously, we are to lean on God's Word.

The key is refusing to put such weight on ourselves that we think we're going to blow it if we don't say exactly the right words or pick the perfect verse.

In fact, we couldn't make the situation better if we tried. So we should let go of that responsibility. It's not ours. We've got to love the person first, and know that there is a time for everything. There is a time to share Scripture. There is a time to talk through how the events unfolded in his life. There is a time to cry. There is a time to let him vent while we remain silent.

And there is a time just to love on him and be there with him.

Bernie Herms and I put together this song in my home studio when he was in town for a local concert. Bernie is a brilliant keyboardist and the husband of singer Natalie Grant.

The conception of this song was unusual in that I had the answer first— a chorus that reminds us to love people like Jesus. But I didn't have the questions yet. I usually write verses first, but Bernie helped me develop those as we dealt with two common situations. Almost every believer will encounter one or both heartaches within their families or friendships. The first verse is about divorce and the resultant torn family. The second verse describes a miscarriage. It poses the quandary of how to approach friends who have lost a child.

Three of my close friends in the ministry lost their babies around the time I was writing this song. Even with the truth I know, I still felt myself not wanting to call them because I didn't know what to say. I churned inside as I thought, *"How do I even begin the conversation?"* It took all I could muster just to call each and say, "Man, I'm so sorry this happened, and you know I love you and I'm praying for you." That's all I had to say. The conversation eased into the miscarriage, and I let each friend talk. But it wasn't my job to go in and make sense of the tragedy.

While wading through those moments, I realized my life was finishing the song. The song was only a song, but I was dealing with real life and real friends, so God connected the two for me.

God's blessings continue beyond heartbreak as well. Afterward, there is a fellowship of suffering that my friends will have with other believers who experience similar trauma. God will use their suffering. There will come another layer of blessing because another lady will suffer a miscarriage, and God will use my friend's wife to minister to her. She can love all over her because they've shared in the fellowship of suffering, and there is nothing quite like that. It is indescribable, really. It has to be experienced to be understood.

I'm reminded of the awesome truth of Hebrews 4:15:

> For we do not have a high priest who is unable to sympathize with our weaknesses, but one who in every respect has been tempted as we are, yet without sin.

Christ is our model. He has a fellowship, a connection, with us. God uses that verse to minister to millions of people to let us know we're not out here by ourselves.

I mentioned my friends in ministry who lost children while I was writing this song. I've already introduced one of them in the football story that began this chapter. Reagan Farris and his wife, Beth, lost a child last year. It was devastating to them, but the Lord has ministered to them and through them and has since given them a beautiful, healthy baby boy.

Reagan preached to our congregation one Sunday when Pastor Tim Dowdy was on vacation, and his words on dealing with tragedy and pain were piercingly simple. He said he finally reached a point where he stopped weeping and stopped questioning and said, "God, I don't need to know why. I just know that I love You....And I trust You." Simple faith is so utterly beautiful.

Reagan Farris is 27 years old. How does a man so young acquire such wisdom? By staying in God's Word. By getting on his knees. By being willing to go through the fire with others—just to be there for them.

Reagan began proving himself in high school, back when he was one of my "Timothys." Back when a young football star named Steven Gerald, who had taught Reagan about mercy a few years earlier, received the lesson in return when he needed it most.

On the day Steven's dad died, I spoke with the guys I was discipling and encouraged them to minister to Steven. They had shunned him because they didn't know where to begin. That night, I visited the funeral home because I had to be at college the next day. I can still see it. I see the driveway with the pea gravel. I see the tiny red-brick funeral home with everybody smoking and talking outside.

As I pulled in, I noticed a truck parked to my right. It was Steven's. He was difficult to miss because of his size. He sat slumped on his tailgate, looking down. And there, all around him, were my guys. They weren't flipping through their Bibles. They weren't trying to explain away everything. The more I watched them and the closer I got to them, I saw that they were simply sitting there with him. Nobody was talking. They were just there for him.

All I could think was, *"He will remember this, and this will lead to a time in which they can talk one day. But right now, all they need to do is just love him."*

Just love him like Jesus.

THE GODLINE

The inherent subject of this song is the sovereignty of God. Our theology must begin with the sovereignty of God, and everything else is centered upon it. The proper view for the believer is that there is no such thing as chance, luck, or coincidence. Rather, everything that happens first filters through God's fingers. He either brings it into our lives or He allows it, but either way He is in complete control.

For this reason, the Godline for *Love Them Like Jesus* is the bridge, which is purposely repetitive to drive home the assurance:

> *The Lord of all creation holds our lives in His hands.*
> *The God of all the nations holds our lives in His hands.*
> *The Rock of our salvation holds our lives in His hands.*

My intent is to pronounce who He is—the indescribably awesome God and Creator of the universe—and yet He holds our finite and comparatively meaningless lives in His hands. Then I close the bridge with:

He cares for them just as He cares for you.

The bridge is a reminder that the Lord is in control.

I once heard a speaker say: "Let's say you and I walk out and hear screeching sounds down the street, and we see cars swerving off the road and hear people honking their horns. And then we see what is causing all the commotion—we see a car blazing through traffic. While the reckless car is barreling toward us, I look up and realize that the driver of the car is my wife, and she's headed toward my building. Everyone else will look at her car and say, 'Look at that maniac.' Everyone except me.

"I'm going to look at her car and say, 'I wonder what's going on with my wife?' You see, I know my wife. I don't understand what's going at the moment, but I know her enough to trust that there is a good reason for what's unfolding."

His point was this: We don't always understand what's happening or why God allowed it, but we do know God. And we know that we can trust Him. Again, just because I don't know His purpose doesn't mean He doesn't have one.

Now here's the best part: Whatever happens is for our absolute best because it comes through the best love, the only true love, the love of Jesus.

THE BOTTOM LINE

- Have you ever experienced a time in which you didn't know how to react when a relative or close friend suffered a tragedy? Did you respond at all, or did you shy away? What is the best example of loving someone like Jesus that you have ever witnessed? Why? What is the worst example? Why?

- Has this song or the above chapter helped you understand how better to approach such situations? How?

- The Lord of all creation, the God of all the nations, the Rock of our salvation holds our lives in His hands. If we believe He is sovereign, should that not embolden us to serve as His ambassadors to those who are hurting? What does our petrified inaction in such times say about our view of God?

CASTINGCROWNS.TV

VIDEO CLIP - "Love Them Like Jesus" from the *Lifesong Live* DVD
You've read it! Now go watch & listen to these stories at
www.castingcrowns.tv

As he was getting into the boat, the man who had been
possessed with demons begged him that he might be
with him. And he did not permit him but said to him,
"Go home to your friends and tell them how much the
Lord has done for you, and how he has had mercy on
you." And he went away and began to proclaim in the
Decapolis how much Jesus had done for him,
and everyone marveled.

MARK 5:18-20

PASSING BY

I'll call her Mary.

In her mid-30s, Mary had a teenage son and worked as a security guard at one of the arenas we played at last year. Mary was backstage all day as we prepared for our nighttime concert, and we got to know her in passing. Usually, her security detail was outside the arena, but she specifically had requested backstage duty for Casting Crowns. We learned why after meeting her.

My wife Melanie especially connected with Mary, who months earlier had been unchurched and in a long-term relationship with her live-in boyfriend. She had known very little about Jesus and His Word. Then God began moving, and He started with Mary's son. The teenager plugged into a church down the street from their home and accepted Christ as his Savior. He discovered our music and bought his mother a copy of the CD.

Mary said she was so moved by the songs on the CD, particularly *Who Am I?*, that she also began attending church. Soon, Mary accepted Jesus and turned from her previous lifestyle. She realized living with her boyfriend wasn't biblical and told him he would have to move out, which was difficult because they had been together for so long. But Mary was so convicted by the Holy Spirit that she stood firm.

Mary felt especially torn on the day her boyfriend returned to carry away his belongings. Mary was still a baby Christian and felt she needed some reassurance that she was making the right decision.

"The first time he came back, I went into my room and just prayed and cried," Mary said. "I said, 'Lord, this is so hard. If this is the right thing to do, please just send me a sign.' And that's when *Who Am I?* started playing on the radio."

Coincidence? Good timing? Or did God work in a simple way to help one of His young children? Mary's favorite song playing in direct answer to prayer helped her through that sad day. But then came another moving day.

Guess what? The same scenario played out again when Mary's boyfriend returned a second time to load the remainder of his belongings. Mary still grieved as she watched him walking away. And for a second time, *Who Am I?* began playing on the radio.

Mary cried while telling Melanie her story. She said *Who Am I?* is a spiritual marker for her, an instrument the Lord has used to remind her that He has a purpose and a plan for her life. She asked for inside duty at the arena so she could at least hear the concert. She also was hoping to meet the band, which is not as much of a longshot as Mary may have imagined....

M

I forgot about the song *Set Me Free* for about six years. Originally, I tucked away this song about the Gerasene demoniac of Mark 5:1-13 because what I was hearing in my head was a style I never saw us pursuing. I also got stuck grammatically. My idea was to have the demoniac speaking first and then Jesus speaking to the demoniac, and I couldn't figure out how to make that work. So I put it aside, and it eventually faded from memory.

Only after hearing some really thundering music did I remember the song. I met Dale Oliver, whose musical compositions are used on many fronts. One day he sampled some of his latest work for me: pro wrestling anthems. I'm not a wrestling fan, but apparently the wrestlers love entering the arena to booming heavy metal. It was an odd and unexpected way to unearth *Set Me Free*, which is a straightforward telling of the demoniac's story. Moved by the biblical record, I was compelled to write a song about it.

The story within the story especially convicted me, however.

As in many New Testament accounts of personal encounters with Jesus, the demoniac came into contact with the God-Man as He was headed somewhere else. Jesus accomplished more ministry on the way to do ministry than most of us will ever imagine. Granted, He is the Son of God, but on earth He was imminently available for ministry because He was so attuned to the will of His Father and was perfectly obedient. The journey was the purpose for Him. It wasn't, "I've got to buy some barley so I can eat and get to the next place to do some ministry." No, the guy selling the barley *was* the ministry. It reminds me of a truth that raised my eyebrows as I read Oswald Chambers' *My Utmost for His Highest*:

"We have the idea that God is leading us toward a particular end or a desired goal, but He is not. The question of whether or not we arrive at a particular goal is of little importance, and reaching it becomes merely an episode along the way. What we see as only the process of reaching a particular end, God sees as the goal itself.…God is not working toward a particular finish— His purpose is the process itself. What He desires for me is that I see 'Him walking on the sea' with no shore, no success, nor goal in sight, but simply having the absolute certainty that everything is all right because I see 'Him walking on the sea' (Mark 6:49). It is the process, not the outcome, that is glorifying to God." [1]

Our band strives to model this philosophy. We seek to honor God and lead people to His throne during concerts, but we also recognize that the stage isn't our only field. Potential ministry exists before and after concerts as well, so we try to concentrate on the people around us when we're on the road.

We get to know the workers loading the sound and running the lights. We engage with arena employees. We stop and talk to security personnel. We meet them, learn their names, and ask them about their families. We talk to them about their lives and their beliefs. We witness to them. They have told us that our intentional interaction isn't common among Christian artists—and I understand why, considering everything a concert entails. But I also realize that sometimes we can get so on-task that it's easy to forget our primary task. There are countless opportunities to touch lives between the Green Room and the stage and between the stage and the bus.

For instance, the stage crewmen aren't in sight to most people. They dress in black because they must be invisible when the lights go down so they can perform their jobs. The problem is that, if you're around this business for too long, they easily can become invisible to you, too. You don't even notice them. They're quiet. They've become accustomed to having very little contact with the artists. In fact, when we want to meet them, they often assume we're arena employees because it's so uncommon for band members to notice them. We've prayed with many of them, we've heard their stories, and we've seen God move in stirring ways just because we listened to them and loved on them.

It all stems from reading Bible stories in which Jesus is on His way somewhere yet no one is an inconvenience to Him.

This ministry philosophy isn't always easy. There is a certain amount of notoriety in the music industry, even in Christendom, no matter how much you try to play it down. One of my constant ministries is to Christian teenagers who want to become musicians, and they're often waiting somewhere to meet me. Usually, their ambitions are similar: They want to be in a Christian band, and they want to "take their ministry to the next level."

God has given me so many opportunities just to hang out with these guys.

I try to take each seriously. I understand that God has given me a moment of influence in someone's life in which, if I'm not careful, I could discourage him completely or encourage him in the wrong way.

I remember a guy named Allen in Florida. He sincerely felt that God wanted to use his music, but I could tell he was only repeating what he had heard others say. He said, "Yeah, man, I just want to take our music to the next level and get it out there so people can hear it."

"Well, tell me what you're doing now," I said.

"I'm in my youth group and I lead worship with the students there," he said. "But, man, I see you guys out here, and I just feel like God is calling me to something bigger."

I had heard it before, and I completely understood his desire. But I wondered if he truly understood God's desire.

"Man, if God is calling you to ministry, He's calling you to ministry right now, right where you are," I said. "I think we all struggle with the problem of focusing so much on what we think God may do a year from now that we trip over what He has for us right now. And what God has for you right now are those 30 kids in that youth room every Wednesday night. There is no next level to those 30 kids. They're it. They're where God has planted you and where every bit of your focus and energy and passion should go."

I could tell my words were sinking in. So I drove home my point with how I've approached student ministry.

"Dude, I don't even have a resume," I said. "When I go somewhere, I'm planning to die there unless God moves me. I don't look to leave. I am not sharp enough to make my own decisions. When we go somewhere, we plug in and pour into people and we live like we're going to be there for the rest of our lives, because that is exactly what we're planning to do unless God steps in and directs us elsewhere. We bloom where we're planted. If God moves you to something different later, or if He moves you to something where more people hear you, that's fine. But that's not a next level. That's just what God has for you to do."

Over the last two years, I've had that conversation at least a hundred times with ministers who sense God's call but assume size determines success. Many have responded to these encounters with e-mails sharing how our conversation altered their ministry perspective.

Isn't it awesome the way the Lord works—even backstage?

Changing the way a minister views ministry is changing the way he views 200 or 300 people in his church. Such an impact on God's kingdom is far more important than sitting in the Green Room for an extra 30 minutes or getting on the bus a little sooner. Believe me, it's not easy. Ministry always requires sacrifice. Always. After a concert, I'm spent. Everything is gone from me. I'm toast, spiritually and emotionally. The feelings are similar to those of a pastor after he has preached.

When I leave the stage, it can be so easy to make a beeline to the bus. Even writing this reminds me of the many times I have failed to stop and look for God's windows of opportunity.

Invariably someone is standing in a corner, and I can tell he's waiting on me to walk past. Meanwhile, Satan is whispering in my ear: *You deserve a break. You deserve to sit down. Your throat hurts. Your back is killing you. You should rest your voice for tomorrow.* But Jesus always responds: *Whoa. This guy is why I brought you here tonight.*

The passing-by moments sometimes become the priority. Often, it's easy to see them as only part of the process. God calls them the end.

THE GODLINE

This song is a perfect example of the many times Jesus stopped and ministered to someone as He was on His way somewhere. He consummately fulfilled His Father's will because the only timetable He had—other than setting His face to go to Jerusalem, and, therefore, the Cross—was His Father's, and it was wrapped up in people. He paused to cleanse the lepers, to give sight to the blind and speech to the mute, to heal the woman with the issue of blood, to call each of His disciples.

The demons living inside the Gerasene man in Mark 5 knew exactly who Jesus is. They knew they were powerless in His presence. They saw Jesus approaching and shrieked His name and begged Him to spare them.

But if the Gerasene man retained any of his own faculties, he must have been exulting on some level that the Christ was in his presence. His only hope stood before him.

We know nothing of this man's past, but we can assume that at some point he was in his right mind and had a home, a family, and a job. He had a life, but then suddenly it was gone. He found himself living among corpses—which, if he was Jewish, was further agonizing defilement—and cutting himself with stones.

That's why the Godline is the song's channel, which describes this biblical story's passing-by moment:

As the God-Man passes by,
He looks straight through my eyes,
And darkness cannot hide.

And then comes a repeat of the chorus, this time slightly altered. The demoniac speaks in the chorus the first two times. Now, in the third refrain, Jesus speaks:

Do you want to be free?
Lift your chains, I hold the key;
All power in Heav'n and earth belong to Me.

That's a Godline not only because of its powerful truth but also because the Lord helped me construct the change in speakers. That wasn't easy. I struggled with it for a while—in fact, one of the reasons I shelved the song years earlier was because I didn't know how to pull it off.

But then one day I was working on the song and Jesus passed by...

And changed everything.

THE BOTTOM LINE

- Can you think of ministry opportunities that you regularly pass by on your way elsewhere? Has the Holy Spirit ever prompted you to pause and minister somewhere? Did you obey? What was the outcome?
- Have you ever needed ministry but no one responded? Why? Was it because the need was not apparent or went unannounced? Or was it because people obviously were indifferent or distracted? How did you feel? How did you respond?
- Do you think God is preparing you for some great goal, or do you walk with Him as if you believe the process is more important to Him? What is more important to you—a great goal, or the daily process? Why?

While You Were Sleeping

But you, O Bethlehem Ephrathah, who are too little
to be among the clans of Judah, from you shall come
forth for me one who is to be ruler in Israel,
whose origin is from of old, from ancient days.

MICAH 5:2

As the bridegroom was delayed,
they all became drowsy and slept.

MATTHEW 25:5

(YAWN)

The giant piano was in the exact same spot. The room had the same blue hue, as always, from sunlight streaming through the same stained glass windows. This time, I sat on the piano stool and smiled as I looked around my college chapel.

It was finally over. I was graduating.

After six long and sometimes difficult years, I was one day away from accepting my degree from Florida Baptist Theological College. It's now called The Baptist College of Florida, apparently renamed during the healing process that took place after my departure. It was the Christmas season. I didn't realize it when I sat down at the piano, but God would send me out just as He had brought me in: At the same time of day and on the same piano in the same chapel in which I had written the song *Fear* (*Voice of Truth*) on my first day of college, I would write another song on my last official school day.

It took me nine years to finish it, but, hey, just as I proved with my six-year college career, you've got to start somewhere. What started on that chapel piano was a song called *While You Were Sleeping* that stayed in my head until I honed it and added a third verse for it to appear on the *Lifesong* CD.

It was 1996. I was trying to come up with something new to sing to the Lord for Christmas.

I wanted to compose a new arrangement to the famous hymn O *Little Town of Bethlehem*. I set out to use the hymn's original lyrics but to spin them into my own version with different chords. I didn't even make it to the second verse. I was playing with some chords and realized halfway into the first verse that I was 27 years old and had been singing the song since I was a kid without grasping its meaning.

It's so easy when you're singing carols and hymns to shift into "hymn mode" and barrel through the verses without realizing the depth and context of the words coming out of your mouth—until the music is different. Somehow, tweaking the arrangement casts the song in a different light. I think it is important that we re-explore traditional hymns and soak in some of the tremendous theology that wonderful men and women of God crafted into a song.

Changing the music for *O Little Town of Bethlehem* certainly opened my eyes. So many people consider it a kid's song without even noticing its powerful message. Halfway through the first verse, the whole point of the song hit me:

They missed it!

Bethlehem missed it. They never knew what happened. They had no idea their Messiah, the Savior of the world, had fulfilled the prophecy of Micah 5:2 and was sleeping in a feeding trough in their very village. They slept through the whole thing. Sing the song to yourself as you read these words of sheer poetry:

> *O little town of Bethlehem,*
> *How still we see thee lie!*

Above thy deep and dreamless sleep
The silent stars go by;

The stage is set. Now look what happens next....

Yet in the dark streets shineth
The everlasting Light;
The hopes and fears of all the years
Are met in thee tonight.

I was floored. I tinkered with a few chords on the chapel piano as I mulled the meaning of the words. I began singing, and out came the line, "O Bethlehem, what you have missed while you were sleeping." When I sang it aloud with those chords, it grabbed hold of me. I said silently, "Whoa, this is so different from what I thought it was going to be."

The song came together as I sang through it over time, and the first verse is basically built around the first verse of the old hymn. There are slight changes to bring out the realization that Bethlehem slept through it all. Originally, I added a second verse starting with a line that was my favorite lyric in the entire song. I eventually ditched the verse because it didn't fit with the song's flow as it evolved, but I remember it nonetheless:

And Mary shivers in the cold, trying to keep the Savior warm.
Born among the animals, wrapped in dirty rags, because...
There was no room for Him in the world He came to save.

At first, I had no intention of making the song anything more than it was. The original two verses sufficed. But then I went to work at the bank in my college town of Graceville one night and couldn't let it go. I was all alone in the bank, scrubbing away, when I thought of incorporating our country into the song:

United States of America, looks like another silent night.

Indeed, it was just another night at the bank in my workaday world, and I thought, *"We're doing the same thing. We're missing it. We're missing the Answer. We're missing the Savior. The United States as a whole is going to miss it just like Bethlehem."* Instantly, the new second verse took the song in a radically different direction, a twist like those in an M. Night Shyamalan movie.

I sang it for the first time at our church in Samson. The people weren't ready for where the song went. They were ready for a Christmas carol, but what they heard seemed to really engross them, judging from their reaction and comments. That's when I knew the song had the potential to be special.

Indeed, it has been special, to me if to no one else. I couldn't bring myself to give up on this song because its message is every bit as relevant now as it was 2,000 years ago, hence the verse about America. When Terry Hemmings, the president of Provident Label Group, heard the original version, he commented on that strong message. He saw the same pattern I had seen:

> *We're so far away from Bethlehem in time and distance, and yet we're so close in spiritual condition. Jesus, the Savior born in Bethlehem, is coming back, just as He promised. The Bridegroom is going to return, and so many people are missing Him—again.*

The more I thought about it, the more I realized that the pattern dictated the need for a middle verse between the Bethlehem verse and the America verse. I needed a new second verse to focus on another city and build a progression to get from Bethlehem to America. Terry had the same thought.

"You know, it's such a strong song that it'd be neat if the second verse was about something else," Terry said.

Right then, it hit me. "What about Jerusalem?" It seemed like a natural step in the song's theme, especially when I thought of Matthew 23:37-38:

"O Jerusalem, Jerusalem, the city that kills the prophets and stones those who are sent to it! How often would I have gathered your children together as a hen gathers her brood under her wings, and you would not! See, your house is left to you desolate."

On His way to the Cross, Jesus paused to weep over His beloved people: "I tried to draw you in, but you wanted no part of Me. How can there be any mistaking who I am?"

As with Bethlehem, Jerusalem saw Him in Person, but He wasn't enough. They wanted more. They wanted signs, and He responded with plenty, though not enough to fancy their wandering hearts and itching ears. They had a picture of the God they wanted, but the God they wanted was a political ruler.

The thought reminded me of a statement I heard Patrick Morley make at a men's conference: "There is a difference between the God we want and the God who is." How true. The people of Jerusalem, those whom Jesus came to save, had established their ideal, but Jesus didn't fit the picture. So they're still looking.

Regrettably, they're not alone. Most of America—most of the entire world—is doing the same, which is why the song concludes with us.

I pray for our country. For far too many people, Jesus isn't enough. They want more. They're guilty of profiling—building their own God—and Jesus doesn't fit the profile.

What's more, America has been blessed into agnosticism. I'm not blaming God; it's our fault. We Americans have taken God's immense blessings upon the most Christian nation the world has ever known and allowed these blessings to make us fat and happy. Oh, must we ever be *happy!*

We have constructed compartments of what is most important to us. We have our families, careers, social lives, hobbies, and sports. Overarching all of them is our quest for happiness, the box we labor most intensely to fill. We let temporal concerns shape what we believe is most important in life, but our desire for happiness undergirds it all.

As a minister, I have observed that many people act as if having God in their lives will adversely affect their plans, so they reserve only a small corner for Him every other Sunday. Apparently, they think that getting too close to God necessarily would affect all their other interests, which, of course, He would and should. Surrender is a dirty word to many people. They don't feel comfortable with that notion. They like their independence. They prefer to control their own destinies, which is laughable when you stop and mull that one.

So they compartmentalize. They say, "This is my home life, this is my church life, these are my kids over here, this is my job. Therefore, these are my ethics at home and these are my ethics at work; this is what I believe about this, and, oh yeah, this is my spiritual life."

Have you noticed the incredible fascination with all things spiritual in the mainstream media? It seems like every other issue of the major news magazines deals with some new theory on Jesus or another "spiritual" topic. Hollywood can't make a movie, it seems, without invoking spiritualism on some level. One of the most popular fiction books of recent times is *The DaVinci Code*, which, of course, spins a poppycock yarn of spiritual matters.

Yet many people refer to "spiritual" themes only in the sense of life enhancement. God is viewed only as *enhancement*. He is not viewed as life itself. If anything uncomfortable or inconvenient comes along with this God who doesn't fit within the rest of the compartments, then they just shave Him off.

America has learned to take what it wants from the buffet of religion: We sample a little of this and a little of that, name it whatever we want, and whatever is good for this person is true, and whatever is good for that person is equally true. We've given it big names like moral relativism. I call it unbelief.

What is the answer? The world needs to see the Church living the truth so vividly that everyone can see the difference.

I have just described the America that I see. It also describes the Jerusalem that Jesus saw. And it describes the Bethlehem that didn't see Jesus. That's why I thought the three places interconnected well in the song.

Someone else had a similar thought more than 137 years ago.

An Episcopal priest named Phillips Brooks enjoyed a pilgrimage to the Holy Land, where he helped lead the midnight service at the Church of the Nativity, which marks the traditional site of Jesus' birth.

"I remember standing in the old church in Bethlehem, close to the spot where Jesus was born, when the whole church was ringing hour after hour with splendid hymns of praise to God, how again and again it seemed as if I could hear voices I knew well, telling each other of the Wonderful Night of the Savior's birth," Brooks said.[1]

Earlier that night, he took a horseback ride from Jerusalem to reach Bethlehem. Along the way he stopped at the Field of the Shepherds and gazed at the valley below as Bethlehem's deep and dreamless sleep slowly descended at dusk. He inhaled the moment and kept it to himself for three years, until when back home in Philadelphia, he wrote a five-stanza poem. His organist, Lewis Redner, took the poem and provided the melody for a song to be performed by the children's choir.[2] It was called *O Little Town of Bethlehem*.

It was 1868. He was trying to come up with something new to sing to the Lord for Christmas.

THE GODLINE

If I had to pinpoint one section of the song that I'm certain the Lord gave me, it would be the third verse. It developed during my nighttime cleaning job at the bank.

I sometimes get chills when I sing it:

And while we're lying in the dark,
There's a shout heard 'cross the eastern sky;

For the Bridegroom has returned,
And has carried His bride away in the night.

I cannot wait for His return, can you? In the meantime, I realize my charge is to be salt and light to an utterly dark world.

An evangelist who preached a revival at Eagle's Landing several years ago sized up our country's spiritual state: "America, once the greatest Christian nation on earth, is now a post-Christian nation rapidly becoming an anti-Christian nation."

How far have we spiraled? I believe this same third verse gives an accurate appraisal with what may be the strongest single line on the album:

As we're sung to sleep by philosophies
That save the trees and kill the children.

This line came to me one afternoon after watching a popular talk show host. In one show surfaced two side topics about which she made it clear she was passionate. The first one was cruelty to animals. The second one was the "right" to abortion. Out of the same mouth in the same hour I heard that animals deserved to live and babies didn't, and it never sounded weird to her or to the audience.

Both stances drew applause. I thought, *"How in the world can we not see how backward that is?"* Especially considering the animal whose fate they lamented in the report. Apparently the poor fellow was being mistreated in some kind of test.

It was a lab rat.

THE BOTTOM LINE

- The people of Bethlehem and Jerusalem missed Jesus. But we can show others to Him through our lives and through His Word: Do you know of specific instances in the Gospels when Jesus claimed deity? Are you readily able to point others to those passages and explain them? Do you have one or two favorites?

- Have you compartmentalized your life and reserved for Him only an hour or two on Sunday mornings? Would people at work be surprised to learn what you believe, or is it obvious to them? What leads you to this conclusion?

- Do you see God as enhancement—as Someone who simply makes life better—or do you truly see Him as life? How do you exhibit that belief?

Father, Spirit, Jesus

But you are a chosen race, a royal priesthood, a holy
nation, a people for his own possession,
that you may proclaim the excellencies of him who
called you out of darkness into his marvelous light.

1 PETER 2:9

THE CONTINUATION

Sometimes songs require years to complete. Sometimes God floats one down into your lap.

We were well into recording the *Lifesong* CD when Terry Hemmings heard a worship song and thought of Casting Crowns. He contacted Mark Miller, our producer.

"There is a writer named Chad Cates who has a really powerful worship song, and I know how Mark and the guys in the band really believe in worship with students and the church in general," Terry said. "This song really would be neat to consider."

It was called *The Continuation*, written by Chad with help from David Hunt. The message fits perfectly with our album because the heart of this song matches that of *Lifesong*. It echoes that worship isn't just something we do in a sanctuary on Sunday mornings; worship is life. The original version was a little different lyrically, but the gist of it was that worship is a continuation of our lives and not just something we tack on to the end of the day.

When I read the lyrics and heard the song, I thought, *"This is the theme of the entire record."* So we began working with Chad, massaging a few sections and tweaking some lyrics. Chad's line at the end of the chorus—"Father, Spirit, Jesus,"—became the title.

I was drawn to this song because it is atypical of worship music. It has such a driving chorus and rocking beat that I thought it would serve a unique purpose. As I mulled over how I could use the song, it dawned on me that it would be the perfect opener when I'm leading students.

One of the most important hats of the several that I wear is that of worship leader. I have discovered through years of trial and error that much has to be accomplished in a worship setting, regardless of the age of the audience. This just may be the toughest task I face.

By Sunday morning, people have been neck-deep in their lives for six harried days. Then they wander into this room where I'm onstage. Some of them have been walking with Jesus all week and were praying on the way in. Some of them haven't thought about Him since the last time they were in that very room.

They walk in, sit down, and await my cue—and there I am before them while their hearts are in a million different places. I have come to understand that, if worship happens at all in some hearts, it won't occur until the second, third, or fourth song of the day. It takes that long for many of them to shove everything else to the side and focus on the Lord. Sometimes the first song can be used to draw them in a little more quickly even though it wasn't necessarily written for that express purpose. That's why I often choose a good, upbeat, rocking song; it seems to grab people's attention. I'm not claiming that this is law or should be the approach of every worship leader. This is just what I believe after leading worship for many years. The key is prayerful consideration of how best to usher people to God's throne.

When we put together *Father, Spirit, Jesus*, I figured it would help shake off the frantic week and remind folks, "This is exactly to Whom we're singing— our Heavenly Father, the blessed Holy Spirit, and our precious Savior. This is what it's all about. You were in one place when you walked in the door, but this is where you are now, and all of this is because of Jesus."

Allow me to share three realizations with which I have been blessed simply by leading worship in different locations and cultural settings.

FATHER:

As a worship leader, my job is to not only create an atmosphere of freedom but also an atmosphere of focus on God. If you watch a group of believers during worship, sometimes we act as if we need permission from everyone else in the room to be open and to enjoy worship. Is *it OK if I raise my hands? Is it OK if I clap? Is it OK if I close my eyes and sway?*

I often see people looking around, uncertain of what they're allowed to do. I've also been self-conscious at times. We're a little worried that we might sing too loudly and someone might hear us and think we don't sound so good. As a worship leader, I strive to help create an environment in which all of that is OK—and it also has to be OK just to sit down and put your hands in your lap and love on people that way.

Did that last sentence confuse you? Let me explain.

One of the first churches in which I led worship was Samson (Alabama) First Baptist. Every Sunday, this little lady sat with her hands in her lap and stared at me with a look on her face that was approaching a scowl. It was almost as if she were saying, "What's that guy up to?"

It would distract me. I thought, *"This lady is not worshipping. It's my job to get her to worship. She's going to get this if it's the last thing I do..."* And I would get angry with her, which is a phenomenon that occurs in worship leaders. Some leaders want you to worship, and some just want you to participate so they don't feel goofy in front of everyone. When the congregation is involved, the worship leader naturally feels a little less awkward. I've seen worship leaders scold the crowd. I've even been less than complimentary after thinking, *"Hey, I'm up here all by myself. Y'all need to join in."* But if it's not in people, it's not coming out of them.

So I didn't know how to respond to this lady with the scowl. Then one

Sunday she caught me off-guard. She walked up to me and said, "Brother Mark, I just want you to know that the worship you lead is one of the highlights of my week. I just love the songs and how you lead worship and how you say things, and I worship with you."

After watching her face every week, I would love to have seen a snapshot of mine at that moment.

I walked out of that sanctuary with a little more understanding. Just because people don't do what I do doesn't mean they're not worshipping. It's not about me and how good I feel onstage and whether everybody loves on me and gives me a big hug afterward. What is my goal up there? My goal is not to make every person in the room stand up on the pews and scream their heads off and wave lighters when I sing. The goal is to create an atmosphere in which the little lady up front can worship as she is led and the high school student in the balcony can worship as he is led, and so can everyone in between.

SPIRIT:

The single most powerful tool I use as a worship leader is prayer. I pray a lot during our worship times. We sing a song or two and then I pray. Another song. Another prayer. There is no greater worship of God than prayer.

To me, worship is praying without asking for anything. I've learned that many young believers don't really know how to pray. They think they have to pray like everyone else does and use the words that others use. Or they think they should pray about whatever subject they assume God must be thinking about at the time instead of what's on their hearts. I pray during worship because I've learned that worship teaches us how to talk to Jesus.

A pastor once challenged me in a message: "If you want to find out how selfish you are, don't ask for anything the next time you pray. See how long you pray."

I tried it. I didn't get a good 30 or 40 seconds into the prayer before I instinctively started spouting off requests for help. It showed me something about myself—that I don't love on Him very much in thanksgiving and praise, not just for what He does for me but for whom He is. Worship helped teach me how to talk to God about how awesome He is.

Now, I pray and read Scripture between the songs instead of offering small talk. I try to make the worship time all about the Lord. I've seen a lot of people—including many students and indeed myself—grow in our prayer lives just because our worship times have helped us understand how to pray. Hearing and participating in authentic prayer within a worshipful context not only moved us but also educated us.

JESUS:

I didn't fully grasp this third lesson for a while, but it has been a tremendous help. After all these years, I understand how imperative it is to be so prepared before I reach the stage that I no longer think about the songs—or the execution of the songs—while onstage. I've stopped worrying about how I'm going to sound. That's for rehearsal. I get everything in order then. When it comes time for worship, I merely sing to Jesus and hope others come along.

I've been onstage when my mind was not focused upon leading people to Jesus. I was distracted with how the music sounded or whether I sang well or whether the words were timed properly on the screens or whether the lighting cues were correct. At that point, I was just singing songs. The songs didn't do anything more than just bounce off of the ceiling, and my voice was merely feedback in the speakers. It was empty.

Worship happens in my worship leader's heart only when my heart is where it's supposed to be and I'm loving on Jesus. Whether we're singing aloud, singing silently, reading the words and listening to everybody else—or sitting with our hands folded and an intense look on our faces—the point of it all is Jesus…and Jesus alone.

THE GODLINE

The channel to *Father, Spirit, Jesus* is inspired from 1 Peter 2:9 (see above) and is the song's Godline:

> *Rescued from darkness,*
> *We are walking in marvelous light.*
> *For we are children of the King;*
> *Sing!*

It's a reminder to look at where we were and where we are now, and it's all because of Him. When you consider how far a holy God had to go to lift us out of the mire, it's all the more reason to worship Him in total freedom. To me, the realization that we are now walking in His marvelous light is, in itself, a call to worship.

THE BOTTOM LINE

- What is your picture of meaningful worship? Why?
- Do you see worship as talking to God—or do you seem only to talk *toward* God during worship? Write down your thoughts on what you have learned about worship while going through this book.
- How intentional are you regarding worship? What are some ways to prepare your heart to worship the Lord?

CASTINGCROWNS.TV

VIDEO CLIP - "Father, Spirit, Jesus" from the *Lifesong Live* DVD
You've read it! Now go watch & listen to these stories at
www.castingcrowns.tv

In Me

For the foolishness of God is wiser than men,
and the weakness of God is stronger than men.
For consider your calling, brothers: not many of you
were wise according to worldly standards, not many
were powerful, not many were of noble birth.
But God chose what is foolish in the world to shame
the wise; God chose what is weak in the world to shame
the strong; God chose what is low and despised in the
world, even things that are not, to bring to nothing
things that are, so that no human being might boast
in the presence of God. He is the source of your life
in Christ Jesus, whom God made our wisdom
and our righteousness and sanctification and
redemption. Therefore, as it is written,
"Let the one who boasts, boast in the Lord."
1 CORINTHIANS 1:25-31

ELEVEN DAYS

Lucci sat in the back of the class on one of his first days of college, his face a picture of bewilderment. He had crossed an ocean after living a life and escaping a death that is now part of the history books, and now, in the classroom of a small college in north Florida, he was caught in the heated crossfire of yet another battle.

Hey, what's a little Romanian Revolution when you can fuss over the King James Version?

I'll never forget one of my first encounters with Lucian Brisc, the guy we would come to know fondly as Lucci (LOO-chee). It was the early 1990s at Florida Baptist Theological College, and Lucci was beginning a new life as a student in America after surviving the Romanian Revolution of 1989. He had helped spark the resistance that eventually overthrew the oppressive and violent dictator Nicolae Ceausescu (Chow-CHES-cu), whose brutal 24-year reign collapsed in 11 bloody days.

On Christmas Day 1989, the bodies of Ceausescu and his wife, Elena, were shown on Romanian television following their execution by a firing squad. That Ceausescu was executed on Christmas Day was ironic, considering the revolution began when Lucci was among a small crowd that camped outside the home of a Christian pastor to defend him from arrest.

At 16 years old, Lucci had helped change the world. He literally had dodged bullets to somehow live while so many of his friends and countrymen bled to death around him. He had stood for Christ while Communism fell.

Imagine how he must have felt to arrive in Florida and hear these "Bless God" boys embroiled in the King James debate.

I call them the "Bless God" boys because many of them could be so dogmatic in their philosophies and language—"Bless God, I'll tell you what …"—that they actually took God's name in vain and left no room for Him to work. Lucci looked at them with a loving yet incredulous eye and informed them, in effect: Thy God is bigger than thy box.

It was one of the first days of school. We were in Bible class when a comment from one side of the room drew a short reply from the other side, which drew an even more curt answer from the middle. And the fire erupted.

Lucci raised his hand amid the clamor. In the sweetest spirit and the best broken English he could manage, he provided a taste of his background.

"I've seen God do amazing things in my country. I've seen the Church come together and overthrow Communism. There is great revival going on all over the place over there," Lucci said. "And you're telling me that, because my people in Romania cannot read English, they will never read the true Word of God because they can't read the King James Bible?"

Silence.

Blessed silence.

In a rare instance for some of them, those preacher boys sat quietly with absolutely no response. Let's just say our class conversations were never quite the same after that statement. Lucci was right. Under some of the arguments being proffered, unless a person speaks English and is able to read and absorb King James English, he cannot read the true Word of God. If it's not the 1611 King James English translation, then he's reading garbage. So if he can't read English, then somehow he's simply toast. Never mind that Jesus didn't say "thee," thou," and "thy." He spoke Aramaic, which was translated mostly into Greek, which then was translated into English and other languages.

Don't those other languages have the inerrant Word of God as well? Isn't God big enough to protect His Word, whatever the language?

I would soon learn why Lucci was so equipped to boldly handle classroom confrontations. In his first one, he had stared into the smirking faces of gun-toting Communist police.

M

It was early in my college career and I was doubling as a youth pastor at New Zion Baptist Church. For fun and a chance at great ministry, I auditioned for the Male Chorale, a 20-man group that represented the college and traveled to sing at area churches and events. Alan Jones and I were two of the first freshmen ever accepted into the group. We truly were the young bucks: the average age of all the students was 35, but I was 20 and Alan was 19. Alan and I hit it off, mostly because of his humble, loving spirit. He was the type of guy who becomes your best friend the moment you meet him. He loves Jesus, and it shows.

We started hanging out and talking music. I was a music student who occasionally sang solos at the college, but I was in my infancy as a songwriter. Alan knew I had helped conduct a few youth rallies at school, so one day he approached me along with another fellow.

"I want you to meet a friend of mine," Alan said. "His name is Lucci."

Alan and Lucci had sung together during chapel service, and they asked if I would join them. We talked about forming our own music group and met with seven other guys one night to try to birth this group. Ultimately, only four guys remained. I joined Alan, Lucci, and Alan Pearce to form a quartet called One Voice.

I could write lyrics and sing tunes, but I couldn't play the piano very well and I certainly couldn't play any other instrument. Alan Pearce was an amazing piano player and Lucci was equally talented on the guitar. Teaming with these incredible players pulled ideas and lyrics out of my head that I didn't know were there. We started singing in churches and eventually performed about 60 concerts a year without ever making a phone call to book an event. God used the ministry while we attended college, served as youth pastors, and worked full-time.

Suddenly, my creativity quotient went off the charts. Along with the guys, I tinkered with several new songs, including one called *The Power of Christ in Me*. This was in the early 1990s. Almost 15 years later, the song made it onto our *Lifesong* CD under the title *In Me*. It testifies to God's using those of us who are foolish, weak, and lowly to build His vast kingdom.

The song is radically different musically than the original, which included a bridge that no longer exists. Because of my struggles with ADD and dyslexia, the bridge tied into Paul's thorn-in-the-flesh verses about his limitations in 2 Corinthians 12:

> *Just like Paul prayed that the Lord would take his thorn away,*
> *I've prayed that prayer so many times.*

But I've found that the one thing that was holding me down
Was the one thing He could use.

I began singing the song with One Voice as for the first time I shared publicly that I had dyslexia. Hearing youth speaker Dave Edwards admit his dyslexia had emboldened me, so this was a very humbling and scary era in my walk. I look back now and praise the Lord for His work of healing and equipping. I thank Him for laying my music foundation through such brilliant and godly men as my One Voice buddies.

And I thank Him for showing me just how small my troubles are by allowing me to serve alongside Lucci and hear his testimony more than 150 times. His story is at the heart of the song's lyrics, and his heart is foremost in my mind when I sing the song now.

Lucci grew up in one of the few Christian families in his Romanian hometown of Timisoara. Every year, he was the only Christian kid in his school. His principals in middle school and high school were hardline Communists; Lucci would share his faith with students and subsequently be told to stop. The kids dubbed him with a new nickname: "The Preacher."

By the time Lucci was in middle school, Ceausescu's personal Gestapo-like police force, called the Securitate (secura-TAH-tay), would enter schools and go to each classroom to ask: "Is anyone here a Christian?" Sometimes they also asked, "Is anyone here a *Repenter?*" using the derisive name they ascribed evangelical Christians. When they reached Lucci's room and asked the question, they were met with silence. Lucci's friends lowered their heads to glance at him and whisper, "Raise your hand. That's who you are."

Lucci swallowed hard and slowly raised his hand. The Securitate surrounded him and insulted him, teasing him and calling him names. These were adult men with guns, and they were trashing this little kid in his classroom.

Lucci's fellow students erupted in laughter while Lucci sat petrified and humiliated. But then something unfamiliar followed.

After the Securitate had their intimidating fun, one by one Lucci's classmates secretly approached him.

"I cannot believe you had to go through all of that," they said. "I can't believe you didn't change your mind and deny God in the face of all they were doing. Tell me about this Jesus."

Thereafter, Lucci was even more emboldened to share his faith, though he repeatedly was warned to stop. Once again, God was using the foolish to confound the wise, the lowly and despised—the things that are not—to nullify the things that are.

Then came a day that changed Lucci's life and sparked a fire that would help change the world.

A few years later, the high school principal called Lucci to his foreboding office. Just as in America, the trip to the principal's office put Lucci face to face with the most imposing figure on campus. Only this was worse: The principal was known for his violent outbursts.

The principal never invited Lucci to sit. Instead, he stood in front of his desk with his back facing Lucci as he mocked and belittled Christians.

"I understand you're talking about Jesus," the principal said.

No answer.

In one violent turn, the principal wheeled in his tracks and punched Lucci with full force in the face, knocking the adolescent to the floor. The principal screamed, "Don't you ever do this again! Don't you ever talk about your faith again!"

As he checked his face for blood, something happened inside Lucci. He was no longer scared. Instead, he became angry. He experienced something he had never felt.

"I'm so sick of this," Lucci thought. *"Why is it that I try so hard to share Jesus and I get beat on all the time?"*

In a flash, he remembered something his mother told him when he walked out the door of his home every morning: "Don't forget who you are. Don't forget Whom you come from."

Then she always would read Scripture to Lucci. One passage that especially spoke to him and he remembered was Isaiah 41:10-11:

> *Fear not, for I am with you; be not dismayed, for I am your God; I will strengthen you, I will help you, I will uphold you with my righteous right hand. Behold, all who are incensed against you shall be put to shame and confounded; those who strive against you shall be as nothing and shall perish.*

Lucci said recalling the Scripture brought a resolve he could not explain. He would never back down. He would never deny his Lord. He would become even more adamant about sharing his faith.

Less than a year later, Lucci was still the only believer who would speak of Jesus in school. In late 1989, the government moved to deport Laszlo Tokes, the pastor of a Reformed church in Timisoara. He faithfully preached despite increasing persecution and also had publicly spoken against Ceausescu. Lucci and his family were members of Timisoara First Baptist Church, pastored by Peter Dugulescu, who became friends with Tokes as they endured constant persecution by the government.

Before the Securitate arrived at Tokes' apartment, Lucci and several friends gathered there to pray on December 15. They joined a small crowd of Tokes' parishioners.

"We're not going to let this happen," the crowd told Tokes.

"You don't need to do this," he answered. "You need to be safe. Go home." The small crowd, and Lucci, refused.

Then came the impossible. The pastor looked outside his window a short while later to see that dozens of people had joined the group. Minutes later the crowd was even larger. Before the end of the day, there were thousands of people surrounding the pastor's home, sensing the time was right to stand up to

Ceausescu's tyranny. Many couldn't have cared less about the pastor's faith. They were famished for liberty.

"I remember that while we all were gathered out there somebody stood on a box and yelled, 'Freedom! This is the day for our freedom!' I had never heard that spoken aloud," Lucci said. "Everyone looked around in amazement, all at once wondering the same question: *'Can you do that? Can you say such things?'*"

Amid the simmering cauldron began a nighttime candlelight prayer vigil that ended in blood two days later.

On December 17, Ceausescu ordered the Securitate to turn on the gathered masses.[1] They fired into the crowd, killing dozens. Lucci had never heard a gunshot before because Romanian citizens were not allowed to own guns. He could hear bullets whiz past as people dropped all around him. Daniel Gavra, one of Lucci's friends from the Baptist church, was at the front of the crowd and immediately was shot in the leg. It later was amputated. Daniel's girlfriend from another church was shot and killed.

Chaos ensued. As people lay dead or bleeding to death, the throng's only recourse at first was to fight back by throwing stones and canned goods taken from nearby stores.

As the confrontation continued, the adults would not let Lucci fight, so he helped make Molotov Cocktails. He didn't know what they were called then, but he assembled the makeshift bombs (a bottle with a flammable liquid and a burning wick extending from the top of the bottle, intended to explode into flames upon contact).

Eventually, government forces detained many protesters, including Lucci and several other young people from his church. As turmoil reigned, he was detained only briefly. Once released, he scurried back to his family's home in time to discover that in some parts of the city the Securitate was going door to door and executing those deemed to be enemies of the state. Lucci's family quietly hunkered down and cried out for God to keep them safe.

Eventually, the revolution erupted full force in the city square, and God was right in the middle of it all.

For Lucci, the highlight of those tumultuous days came when his own pastor, Peter Dugulescu, led almost 200,000 people in reciting the Lord's Prayer. After 45 years of Communism, Romanians publicly petitioned God.

So sweeping was the revolt that much of the national army eventually turned against the government. They helped overwhelm the Securitate, who had become nothing more than urban terrorists committing random violence before their demise.

Casualty reports from the revolution vary, but it is believed that more than one thousand people died and more than 3,000 were wounded. Ceausescu and his wife tried to escape the country but were captured and executed after a hasty "trial" in which they were accused of ordering the deaths of more than 60,000 of their countrymen during their regime.[2]

Lucci and his parents were reunited with his three brothers and their families. The two pastors, Tokes and Dugulescu, enjoyed international acclaim for sparking the downfall of Communism first in Timisoara, then in the capital of Bucharest and other cities, and eventually throughout Eastern Europe. Lucci had been in the thick of it, joining the initial dissenters in the first small group.

Today, Lucci is 32 years old and recently wed a beautiful Romanian bride. He remains heavily involved in missions work in his homeland. Lucci and Alan Pearce live in Dothan, Alabama and help fledgling Christian musicians. Alan Jones is a minister at a church in north Florida.

As I reflect upon Lucci's story and my time singing with him in One Voice, I see his monumental impact upon my life. His story clearly surfaces in the second verse:

If You ask me to run,
And carry Your light into foreign land;
If You ask me to fight,
Deliver Your people from Satan's hand...

That's exactly what Lucci did. He fought and helped deliver his people from Satan's hand in Romania. And then he brought his unique light to America.

How did Lucci wind up on our little Florida campus?

The same sovereign God who sustained him through the school principal's punch and the dictator's madness also called him into ministry when the storm quelled. Lucci told Pastor Dugulescu that he sensed God's beckoning, and his church partnered with First Baptist Church of Perrine in Miami, Florida to sponsor his education. They chose to send him to a Bible college to learn theology, and they selected Florida Baptist Theological College.

That's where he quickly learned just how worked up Americans also can become—not to overthrow an oppressive regime, mind you, but to argue over Bible versions.

The young man whom God used to help take down Ceausescu traveled thousands of miles to America only to hear that we didn't know whether his faith was based upon a legitimate translation. So he had to say something in protest.

He just had to.

THE GODLINE

The song's original chorus was three lines long:

When I'm weak, He makes me strong.
When I'm blind, He shines His light on me.
And I'll never get by, living on my own ability.

I sang those lines twice to comprise the chorus, which I considered the song's weak point. When I decided to include it on the Lifesong CD, I immediately focused on the limping chorus. Part of my personal testimony is that I have learned God doesn't need me but wants me. I decided to strengthen the chorus with that thought, so I added:

How refreshing to know You don't need me.
How amazing to find that You want me.
So I'll stand on Your truth, and I'll fight with Your strength,
Until You bring the victory, by the power of Christ in me.

Toward the end of the song, I decided to throw in a bit of a twist. As the music lowers, my son, John Michael, sings the first three lines of the chorus. I thought having a child sing those particular lyrics would even more vividly drive home the point.

As he sings, "When I'm weak, He makes me strong," I'm reminded of the parallels to the children's song *Jesus Loves Me*. It brings in an element of child-like faith and evokes a child's courage. Children will dive into anything—especially if they know their daddy is going to catch them. They'll jump off of a cliff if they think he'll be on the other end. It's a reckless kind of faith that, unfortunately, most of us grow out of over time. Having a child sing the chorus helps us capture the idea that we need to be like we used to be.

I recently read a book entitled *The Barbarian Way* by Erwin Raphael McManus. The gist of his message is that we Christians have grown up and our faith has become civilized. The way I see it, civilized, grown-up Christians don't kill giants and don't walk on water. They have too many charts and pie graphs to figure out the pros and cons before they'll do anything, rather than simply jumping out there in Daddy's arms.

That one little moment in the song, listening to those lyrics through a seven-year-old voice, can have a profound impact on adult hearts. Everywhere we perform, invariably someone brings up *In Me* and asks whether that's my son who is singing. One man told us he had to pull his car to the side of the road because he began weeping after hearing John Michael's chorus.

It also makes John Michael's daddy awfully proud. Every time I hear him sing it, I can't help but smile.

There's another twist, however: As powerful a message as the chorus conveys, it's still not the song's Godline.

Remember the original bridge that was based on the 2 Corinthians 12 passage? I ditched that long ago. I replaced it with lines that I know the Lord gave me, so the bridge is the Godline:

To reach out with Your hands,
To see the world through Your eyes,
To love with the love of a Savior;
To feel with Your heart,
And to think with Your mind,
I'll give my last breath for Your glory.

It's a declaration of what I'm willing to do, but it's also a realization that there is nothing that I can do on my own. There is a balance between two truths that run parallel, like train tracks. I am saying, "This is what I'll do, but I cannot do it by myself." A believer should fully understand both. We must realize and believe that He's going to be there when we jump—but we still have to jump.

Carman had a line in one of his songs on faith that always zinged me: "Stepping out on nothing and finding something there." That is a cool line. That's the life of faith. When we make bold proclamations such as, "I'll be a warrior for Christ," we still should understand that He alone will make it happen.

How many of us are willing to take such a stance? How many of us unabashedly live a life of faith? How many of us can say, "I'll give my last breath for Your glory" and truly mean it?

No?

Well, I want you to meet a friend of mine. His name is Lucci.

THE BOTTOM LINE

- Name the thorns in your life from which you have asked God to deliver you:_____

  _____

  _____

  _____

- Has God used your thorn(s) in any way to impact the world and His Kingdom? How? Has the struggle been worth it in your eyes?
- Do you consider yourself abandoned to Christ? Why or why not? Does the fruit of your life bear out your response? If you're not where you want to be in your walk with Jesus, what is holding you back?

Prodigal

And he arose and came to his father. But while he
was still a long way off, his father saw him and felt
compassion, and ran and embraced him and kissed him.
And the son said to him, 'Father, I have sinned against
heaven and before you. I am no longer worthy to be
called your son.' But the father said to his servants,
'Bring quickly the best robe, and put it on him, and put
a ring on his hand, and shoes on his feet. And bring the
fattened calf and kill it, and let us eat and celebrate.
For this my son was dead, and is alive again; he was
lost, and is found.' And they began to celebrate.

Luke 15:20-24

COMING HOME

Have you ever noticed that no names are mentioned in the story of the prodigal son? There is good reason. There's not enough room for all who qualify.

My name would be there, printed in neon scarlet. Yours would be there. Everyone would need an extra-bold Sharpie and room to print legibly.

The story is fascinating for many reasons, not the least of which is that it is a snapshot of Scripture as a whole. God's Word is living and active and sharper than any two-edged sword, and it cuts straight to the heart. (Hebrews 4:12) Scripture can hit you in a different place every time you read it because it breathes, and this is so true of the story of the prodigal son as told by Jesus in Luke 15.

I've been every person in this parable. Let me outline the different parts I've played.

I've been the kind of prodigal who was out there running and didn't even know it. I had drifted away, and what previously had been important to me was no longer a priority. Other interests had pressed to the fore. One Sunday my hands were lifted and I was led by the Holy Spirit in prayer after a week spent with Jesus, and the next Sunday I realized my hands were in my lap and I was looking around at other people and thinking, *"That guy is probably not even real. His hands are up in the air, and he's kind of fake."*

When I'm not walking with Jesus as I should and I see someone else worshipping, I often wind up thinking, *"Either they're a fake or I'm missing something."* It's so much easier to assume that others are fake. It doesn't hurt as badly.

In those moments, I have to pause and ask myself, "Wait a minute. How did I get here from there?"

Everything was going fine. I was consistently living by faith. But somewhere—and I'm not sure exactly where—I began walking in my own strength. I'm a hundred miles away from where I was, and all I remember is a couple of small compromises. Compromise is like a snowball rolling downhill: It just gets bigger, faster, and easier.

Then God has to break through again. He has to point His bright light into the musty crevices of my heart and whisper, "Hey, where have you been? Just a few days of not being in My Word has turned black-and-white matters into gray."

It reminds me of swimming in the ocean one summer. I was in the water and looked up to see Melanie straight ahead of me on the shore, and I waved at her and the kids. I continued swimming, but in just a few minutes I looked again and couldn't see Melanie because I was halfway down the beach. I had drifted and didn't even realize it.

That is true of the prodigal story. He didn't know his life was a mess until all the money was gone. We all have been in his shoes to some degree. We've all tried to live in our own strength for a certain time, performing all the tasks, good deeds, and Christian acts in our own power. After a while, when there is no daily walk with Jesus, our efforts hollow out. Next comes the thud, and great is the fall.

I've been that kind of prodigal many times.

On other occasions, my prodigal nature wanted to avoid a reckoning: I have realized, "I need to go to God with this sin, but I don't want to, because I don't want to deal with the reality that I've done this."

I've also been the prodigal who experienced forgiveness. I have needed forgiveness from God or other people but was reluctant to seek it, thinking I would face an awkward and terrible scene. But He already was waiting for me.

At the same time, I've been the brother who can't stand to see the wicked prosper. I kept a scorecard of all of my brothers and sisters who weren't sacrificing as much as I was and yet were still impressing everyone and living happily ever after. These emotions so needled me that I turned bitter. Boy, have I ever been the surly brother....

And then I've been the father.

There have been times when others have approached me with a broken heart, looking for forgiveness, but I had the goods on them. I had all the power to forgive or to condemn. I was right and knew it. I had been wronged, and they knew it. They owed me—an apology at least. I've experienced situations in which others had to come humbly to me with their heads on the chopping block. I had to make the choice to forgive them. Forgiving them meant relinquishing my right to revenge and permanently laying it aside, and sometimes pride makes that awfully difficult to do.

I've been every person in this story. That may explain why this song became the story of the prodigal, because initially I was only thinking of myself. When I came up with the first verse, I was mulling over my own life. You don't have to walk away and become a drug-dealing womanizer to be a prodigal.

I know who I am and what I'm like when I'm walking with God, and I know who I am and what I do when I'm living for myself. It's not like I go out and kill puppies, but my walk develops a definite hollowness. It becomes superficial. It becomes Pharisaic. I still may engage in ministry and sing songs, but my efforts are tainted by a lack of substance that diminishes my authenticity.

That's why my songwriting features such a black-and-white perspective. I'm at the point where I don't tolerate gray areas in my walk with Jesus because I've learned that gray is Satan's favorite color. Gray areas are the breeding ground of compromise. I'm not saying that everyone who writes songs needs to write them like I do. I'm merely reporting how my songs emerge because of where I am in my walk with God, and I can't play games with Him.

When I'm not living like I should, I can't even ask the blessing over my food. It's like God is saying, "What is this? What are you bringing to Me? You're going religious on Me." I have such a bad taste for that kind of living that when I'm there—and I'm there far too often—I have to approach God and repent immediately. I've learned that living out in a faraway land and doing your own thing doesn't necessarily mean you're doing something on the church's bad list. It may mean that you're doing good work—but doing it without Him. Either way, it's prodigal living.

This song has been the bane of my existence for quite some time. I've been writing it for four years, and musically it has transitioned through at least six versions. Eventually, we decided to use a really cool musical arrangement with which I had help from Michael Tait of dcTalk and Chad Chapin. We tracked all the music first, and then I prepared to walk into the booth to record the vocals.

It would be just a matter of minutes before the song changed again.

Something wasn't right. The verses, channel, and melody had stayed the same from the start, but I had never been able to write a chorus that lived up to the other components. I realized that the chorus was getting a little too happy for the subject. I stepped up to the microphone and sang along with the track, which was a wonderful rock version.

As soon as I sang the last note, I knew I had not recorded the song locked inside my head. And I couldn't just let it go. I looked through the recording studio window at Mark Miller, who knew this song had haunted me for years as I second-guessed it repeatedly.

"Mark…." I said, a lilt in my voice.

"Oh, no," he answered. "You've got to be kidding."

"Dude, this isn't happening," I said. "I ain't feeling it, man. We're lost."

He shook his head and smiled. "If we re-write this song, you have to write another song for this track, because this track is awesome."

The music was terrific, but it was different. Everything was different. The melodies were different. It wasn't what I was hearing in my head.

Mark Miller broke a pregnant pause: "What do you want to see happen with this?" he asked. "The very first time you ever sat down in the studio with me, you played something on the piano, and it was so honest and so real. Play that to me again."

I pulled up to the keyboard and started plunking out my spare version. When I finished, he said, "Mark, that's the song." And the band all agreed. When I had first shown them the new version, they loved the music and the "rock" feel of it, but they made clear their opinions: "Dude, it's just not *Prodigal*. It's a great song, but it's not *Prodigal*."

I felt better that I wasn't alone in my opinion. I played the original version for Mark, and that is what made the CD, except for one minor problem. I didn't have a chorus for it. That was a tad cause for concern.

I was still sitting at the piano when I said, "The chorus just isn't right. It ought to say something like this," and I started playing and singing. What I sang off the top of my head is what you hear now. I had never thought of the chorus before that moment.

I said, "It ought to be something like…

Daddy, here I am again,
Will you take me back tonight?

Out of the corner of my eye I saw Mark point to Sam Hewitt, our engineer, and say, "Get this." Sam hit the recording button, and Mark told me to keep singing. I sang the chorus one more time, and they captured it:

Daddy, here I am again,
Will you take me back tonight?
I went and made the world my friend,
And it left me high and dry;
I drag your name back through the mud
That you first found me in.
Not worthy to be called your son,
Is this to be my end?
Daddy, here I am,
Here I am again.

Mark smiled. "That's your song," he said. "You just need to let it be what it is and stop trying to make it the biggest song on the record."

I know why I grappled with this song. It always has been special to me because the story is about me, and I didn't want to lose it as some weird B-side single that no one ever hears. The message is too strong. I was trying to make the song huge when the lyrics were the point of the whole thing.

It had been a difficult process. Red Smith was a famous New York sportswriter who explained, "Writing is easy. You just open a vein and bleed." After this song, I knew what he meant.

Fittingly, I close the song with a soft lament that echoes in the background. Maybe you've been trying to figure out what I'm singing, because we didn't put these lyrics in the CD liner notes. They summarize the song's story—and the laborious journey through its composition:

I am beaten, I am torn...I'm not running ...I'm not running anymore.

THE GODLINE

The song's channel so resonates with me. It pictures the person who finally realizes how woefully short of God's holiness he falls—and his proper response of contrition.

And I've held out as long as I can;
Now I'm letting go and holding out my hand.

I've used this illustration with my students before: Imagine a man hanging onto a rope over a pit of alligators. He has the rope in one hand and a sword in the other hand to fight off the alligators. The alligators are nipping at his feet, getting closer by the second as he's frantically fighting with all of his might. Finally, he thinks to himself: *"You know what? If I can just get a better grip on this sword, I can really fight them off."* So he lets go of the rope to get a really good grip on his sword so he can fight off the alligators....

Does that make any sense?

Many of us are guilty of such flawed thinking. The process begins with the Holy Spirit convicting us and telling us, "Look how far you've drifted." At the same time, Satan slinks in and whispers, "That's it. You've blown it. God is not going to love you anymore unless you fix this."

So we let go of grace and everything that got us where we are, and we say, "I've got to make this better." We begin hacking away, trying to make the bad stuff go away while also performing extra helpings of good deeds, and it spirals into a big tailspin. At that point, we're practicing religion and wondering why it's not working: "Well, I'm doing all the stuff. I read my Bible. I worship. I serve. I minister. I share my faith, and nothing is working. Why is this not working?"

Because now it's just religion. And Daddy wants a relationship.

THE BOTTOM LINE

- **Prodigal:** Can you detail a period of time in which you insisted on living in your own strength and on your own terms? What was the outcome? How did the Lord redeem you or restore you?
- **Father:** What is your typical reaction when you are in a position to forgive someone who wronged you? Are you maintaining an unforgiving spirit toward someone now? In light of what Scripture teaches, would you say your attitude is godly? Why or why not?
- **Brother:** Have you ever found yourself resenting others for the blessings in their lives? What was the source of your resentment? How did you respond? What is the proper response?

And Now My Lifesong Sings

But God shows His love for us in that
while we were still sinners, Christ died for us.
ROMANS 5:8

HALLELUJAH

I once was lost, but now I'm found;
I once was lost, but now I'm found;
So far away, but I'm home now;
I once was lost but now I'm found.
And now my lifesong sings...

Darrell Jenkins came in out of the cold one Sunday morning, leaving behind a world of drugs and alcohol, Friday paychecks and Saturday morning wipeouts, and learned that God had prepared a place for him.

Finally, he knew he had an eternal home—good news for someone who once lived in a refrigerator box behind his favorite bar.

Eighteen months before I moved to Eagle's Landing, Darrell woke up on a Sunday and went looking for a church. That's not so unusual in the Bible Belt. But it is unusual for someone like Darrell. He had destroyed almost every relationship he knew, including his first marriage, and was busily destroying himself. He worked as a roofer to earn just enough money to party away the weekend. He had been in and out of jail and could not escape the suffocating culture of a third-world community called Cabbagetown.

Another reason the day was so remarkable was the weather. An ice storm had crippled Atlanta. Much of the metro area was without electricity, and people were burrowed in, but Darrell was compelled to find a church. By this point, he had met a girl named Becky and had moved in with her. Darrell looked outside at the icicles hanging from tree limbs and shrugged.

"I'm going anyway," he told Becky, and they piled into her car and headed down Jodeco Road.

They passed one church. Closed. Then another church. Closed. They approached a third. No cars. No people. They drove until reaching the end of Jodeco, where their decision was made for them. To drive through the traffic light meant entering the parking lot of the county's largest church. People were parking their cars and walking inside. Darrell actually had been visited by members of this church before.

For the first time, he would step foot in Eagle's Landing First Baptist Church.

The crowd was small, the worship center was frigid, and without power they were limited to worshipping acapella while one tuba player kept time. Pastor Tim Dowdy preached for maybe 20 minutes.

Darrell doesn't recall the sermon topic; he only remembers he could not stay seated during the invitation. "I had no choice," he says. "I was already walking up there, and it was like my body had to catch up." There is one Transformer that never loses power, and the Holy Spirit regenerated a crack cocaine user on a morning when everything else was frozen solid.

I learned of Darrell's story when I moved to Eagle's Landing and became a co-worker with someone who told me all about it: Darrell himself.

He left his roofing job to join our operations staff, taking a 50-percent pay cut because as a baby Christian he knew he could not withstand the temptations and pressures of living in his old world alongside his former friends. He gave up everything of his old way of life, married Becky, changed careers, and faithfully attended church.

Almost six years later, Darrell is still vacuuming the halls, cleaning up after sick kids, and repairing leaks for our church and school. He can hardly talk about Jesus without crying. He is one of the most popular people in our family—so popular that, when he told his story during school chapel, the kids interrupted the introduction and began clapping upon mention of his name. Darrell candidly told them how far God had brought him and even showed a video of his former haunts, including the bar's rear dock where he had slept in the refrigerator box.

Then he closed with Scripture that perfectly pictures God's work in his life. I used the same verse in the earlier chapter on *Praise You With the Dance* to describe what God does for all of us. Read Psalm 40:1-2 and think of Darrell's perspective:

> *I waited patiently for the Lord;*
> *He turned to me and heard my cry.*
> *He lifted me out of the slimy pit,*
> *Out of the mud and mire;*
> *He set my feet on a rock*
> *And gave me a firm place to stand.*

"Ain't that awesome?" Darrell told the kids in chapel. "That's what He did for me. He took me off the streets and out of the cardboard boxes and put me here to share my story with you to show you that He is who He says He is."

Just that simple. *I once was lost, but now I'm found.*

M

> *I once was blind, but now I see;*
> *I once was blind, but now I see;*
> *I don't know how, but when He touched me,*
> *I once was blind, but now I see.*
> *And now my lifesong sings…*

James Martin was known as the meanest man in north Florida. People said he had a gun in every tree in the woods. His strapping 6-foot-3 frame was made more intimidating by his chiseled Indian face. You just didn't mess with the guy. He was legendary.

Before I became a part-time youth pastor at New Zion Baptist Church in Bonifay, Florida, the Lord transformed James' heart. So monumental was his salvation that it remained the biggest news in the region for months afterward. People literally traveled from miles around to visit the church and hear his story. His reputation was such that they would not have believed it otherwise.

James would tell his story, but he wouldn't use three points and a poem. He wouldn't quote a ton of theology. He didn't know a lot of Bible verses. All he knew was, "I once was lost, but now I'm found. I once was blind, but now I see."

One of the biggest testimonies about James was his smile. It was the most winsome, bright, peaceful smile. Even his eyes smiled. Not many people had seen it before, but when Christ gave him new life, it was there for all to see.

I knew James for about two or three months before I heard anything about his past, and the locals needed several weeks to convince me of his background. I thought they were trying to pull one over on the rookie, because all I ever saw was this guy who loved Jesus and loved everyone around him. He met you and then loved on you. He was like a daddy to Melanie and me. We were just getting started in ministry at our first church, and James helped us beyond measure. I think of him when I sing this song.

Today, James is still in his church and loving on people. He still has that smile. It's been almost 15 years, but James Martin is a church leader regarded by many as something of a spiritual dad. He was one person in his past life, and then he met the Lord Jesus and became someone completely different. He would love to smile and tell you about it someday.

Just that simple. *I once was blind, but now I see.*

M

I once was dead, but now I live;
I once was dead, but now I live;
Now my life to You I give...
Now my life to You I give...
Now my life to You I give...

While I was youth pastor at Center Hill Baptist Church, one of the "stoners" at a local high school was a neo-hippie named Steven White. He literally communicated through Surferspeak. "Heeyyyy, whasssup, duuuude?" he would ask, eyes little more than slits.

One summer, Steven went along for fun to a church youth camp. God saved Steven, who immediately did an about-face. Nothing of his old life ever came back. He wasn't even one of my students; he attended First Baptist Church of Loganville. I knew his story only because of the tainted reputation that had preceded him—and then suddenly everyone met a new Steven. He now is a worship leader in Loganville and has his own band called The Sullivan Street Band.

I've known Steven for nearly a decade, and I vividly recall how amazed everyone was to see how he never looked back. He totally changed, and he attracted people all the time because he wasn't deep. He didn't recite a bunch of theological terms describing the change but said only, "The old man is gone. I'm a new man. This is who I am."

Just that simple. *I once was dead, but now I live.*

M

The song *And Now My Lifesong Sings* is part of a trilogy I had intended to record for the *Lifesong* CD. The trilogy would begin with *Prodigal* and conclude with *And Now My Lifesong Sings*. I decided to hold the middle song, which is about struggling with forgiveness, because I didn't feel it was ready. It likely will appear on our next CD.

I'm happy with how the *Lifesong* CD concludes, however, because in my mind *And Now My Lifesong Sings* is the song of the Prodigal Son—the worship song that he sang after he returned home.

I also like how the song closes the CD by making sure everyone's attention is where it belongs:

> *Hallelujah.*
> *Hallelujah.*
> *Let my lifesong sing to You...*

THE GODLINE

For those of us who have tasted the new birth, we should remember that we all were once prodigals. We all were lost, and we're found only because Christ "found" us. We were dead, and we're alive only because Christ's life resuscitated us.

So the words "And now my lifesong sings" is this song's Godline. I want to drive home the point that the only reason I have a lifesong, the only reason I'm able to sing, the only reason I can serve Him and even understand His Word is because I'm alive now when once I was dead. Otherwise, there is no lifesong.

I didn't wake up one day and decide that I was going to live for Jesus in my own strength. I cannot honestly say, "I'll tell you what, I'm just going to do it all—I'm going to sing, I'm going to worship, I'm going to impress God with how I live."

Another line also is special to me: "I once was blind, but now I see." It is lifted from one of the Bible's most compelling encounters. In John 9, Christ heals a man born blind. The Pharisees gathered and called for the healed man, and his testimony before them was, "All I know is that I once was blind and now I see." That's all he understood.

I am gripped by the simplicity of burning everything else away and boiling down God's redemption to this: It wasn't anything I did. It wasn't something I realized one day after glancing heavenward. I didn't read about it and figure out that I needed God. He did it all. *I once was lost, and now I'm found.* I didn't "find" Jesus. I was blind—I couldn't see Him—and now I see. I was dead, and now I live. Ephesians 2:1 says that we were dead in our transgressions, and dead people don't do anything. No one comes to the Father unless the Spirit draws him. (John 6:44) This song is just a simple declaration of my realization that God did this for me.

If all of this sounds alien to you, then I encourage you to read the book of John. Ask God to open your eyes to His truth. Afterward, if you truly desire a relationship with God, then His Holy Spirit is working in your heart because only He can produce that desire. Then I invite you to pray along these lines:

> *Heavenly Father, I realize I'm a sinner and need a Savior. I acknowledge that You sent Your Son, Jesus Christ, to die on the Cross for my sins. I ask You to forgive my sins and I accept Jesus into my heart as my Savior. I long for the eternal life only You can provide, and I pledge to live for You the rest of my life. Thank You for Your forgiveness and love. In Christ's name, Amen.*

Just that simple. If you truly mean it, you too can sing: *I once was lost, but now I'm found.*

THE BOTTOM LINE

- Has there ever come a time in which you asked Jesus Christ into your heart as your Savior? Are you placing your trust in Christ alone for eternal life? Do you believe He is the Son of God sent to die on the Cross for your sins? Do you believe He is your *only* way to Heaven?
- If you have prayed to receive Christ, has there been a life change? In what ways? Be specific. Use the space provided in the next chapter to

record the events surrounding the day the Lord gave you a new lifesong.

- Are you more interested in the things of this world or the things of God? Are you Kingdom-minded, or do most of your pursuits involve personal fulfillment?

Journal

Therefore, if anyone is in Christ, he is a new creation.
The old has passed away; behold, the new has come.
2 CORINTHIANS 5:17

MY LIFESONG

My sincere hope is that the stories behind our songs have encouraged, inspired, strengthened, convicted, corrected, emboldened, and motivated you. The Word of God and His Holy Spirit are all you will ever need to live a life of righteousness and obedience before the Lord, but it also is helpful to see evidence of how God is working among His people.

That's why I wrote this book. And that's why there is no story more important than yours. One of your most effective tools in telling others about Jesus is your testimony. People sometimes try to dispute Bible facts; they cannot dispute how God has changed your life.

Whether you share your testimony often or struggle to find the words, it is a helpful exercise to write down your testimony. It will remind you of events you have forgotten, reveal how God has filled in the blanks in your life, and encourage you with the Lord's unfathomable faithfulness. Reflection is a salve for the soul. (Nehemiah 9-10) Grab a pen and let your lifesong sing.

_____

_____

NE✗T STANZA...

Now that you've recorded your lifesong, I ask you to undertake another helpful exercise. Just answer this question:

What do you want the next verse of your life to say?

Maybe you feel as if you've never really completed the first verse. Maybe there are a few scratches on your record and you are stuck on a mundane chorus that is repeating itself over and over. Maybe your strength is so small that the words are caught in your throat.

Maybe it's time for a fresh start.

Let me share with you one of the most inspiring passages in all of Scripture:

> *Now I saw a new heaven and a new earth, for the first heaven and the first earth had passed away. Also there was no more sea. Then I, John, saw the holy city, New Jerusalem, coming down out of heaven from God, prepared as a bride adorned for her husband. And I heard a loud voice from heaven saying, "Behold, the tabernacle of God is with men, and He will dwell with them, and they shall be His people. God Himself will be with them and be their God. And God will wipe away every tear from their eyes; there shall be no more death, nor sorrow, nor crying. There shall be no more pain, for the former things have passed away."*
>
> *Then He who sat on the throne said, "Behold, I make all things new." And He said to me, "Write, for these words are true and faithful."*
>
> *Revelation 21:1-5 (NKJV)*

The Savior who makes all things new is longing to continue a fresh work in you. As you prayerfully seek the Lord's heart, I encourage you to set goals for the remainder of your life. What are your hopes? Your dreams? If nothing in your life was saying "no" to you, what would you do, where would you go, and how would you minister? Don't dwell upon past failures, current obstacles, or fear of what the future may hold. Remember, Jesus Christ is the same yesterday, today, and forever. (Hebrews 13:8)

Take a few moments to record your grandest goals, desires, and passions in Christ. Just as Jesus told John in the Revelation, so now I say to you: Write!

And then believe and act. For His words are true and faithful!

_____

_____

_____

_____

_____

_____

_____

_____

_____

_____

_____

NOTES

Who Am I?

1. John Piper, "The Debtor's Ethic: Should We Try to Pay God Back?" *Future Grace*, (Multnomah Publishers, Inc., 1995), pp. 31-39.

Glory

1. Oswald Chambers, "August 21" devotional, *My Utmost for His Highest*, edited by James Reimann, (Oswald Chambers Publications Association, Ltd., 1992).

Does Anybody Hear Her?

1. Ed Tandy McGlasson, "Developing Rites of Passage," *The Difference a Father Makes*, (Ampelon Publishing, 2004), pp. 60-61.

2. Dr. Robert Blum and colleagues, "Lost Children or Lost Parents of Rockdale County?," in "The Lost Children of Rockdale County," PBS Online and WGBH/Frontline, <http://www.pbs.org> [path: /wgbh/pages/frontline/shows/georgia/isolated/blum.html], 1999.

3. Ibid.

Set Me Free

1. Oswald Chambers, "July 28" devotional, *My Utmost for His Highest*, edited by James Reimann, (Oswald Chambers Publications Association, Ltd., 1992).

While You Were Sleeping

1. Author unknown, "O Little Town of Bethlehem," <www.cyberhymnal.org > [path: /htm/o/l/olittle.htm], 2005, established 1996.

2. Author unknown, "O Little Town of Bethlehem," <www.ingeb.org> [path: /spiritua/olittlet.html], 2005.

In Me

1. William Horsley, "Romania's Bloody Revolution," in BBC News/World/Europe, <www.news.bbc.co.uk> [path: /2/hi/europe/574200.stm], 1999.

2. Ibid.

Acknowledgements

Do not withhold good from those to whom it is due,
when it is in your power to do it.
PROVERBS 3:27

THANKS, GUYS

To Melanie: You are a treasure in my life. You are the most amazing, talented, selfless servant I've ever known. You keep me focused. You believe in me. Although I often wonder how God is going to make it up to you, I know that you are His greatest blessing to me outside of Jesus. I love you.

To my parents, John and Kay Hall: Thank you for never ceasing to love, encourage, and challenge me even to this day. I wish every teenager could grow up with you guys.

To Mark Miller, Norman Miller, Mike Jay, Terry Hemmings, Dean Diehl, and Steven Curtis Chapman: Thank you for going against the norm and taking a chance on an old youth pastor. I thank God that I am a part of your ministries.

To Tim Luke: Thank you for gathering my attention and thoughts (and then regathering them…Ha!) and helping me put into words what is in my heart.

To my editor Don Pape: Thank you for smoothing out the rough spots.

To my pastor, Tim Dowdy: Thank you for throwing away the rulebook on how ministry is done and letting God be creative in my ministry to students at Eagle's Landing First Baptist Church.

To Reagan Farris and Georgia Sexton: You are the most amazing team I've ever worked with in student ministry. I pray for you guys daily and thank God for your ministry to our students and to me.

Casting Crowns: You guys are my closest friends and I can't wait to see what God has in store for us next. I love you guys.

And finally to all my "Timothys" out there (and you know who you are): I pray that your lifesongs sing to the Father....

THE AUTHORS

MARK HALL

Mark Hall's 36-year-old heart beats for teenagers, which is why he has been called to be a student pastor. He just sings to them to get his points across. Despite the multi-platinum success of his band Casting Crowns, Mark serves on staff at Eagle's Landing First Baptist Church in McDonough, GA. His 400 teenagers still receive his attention every Wednesday night, even if he has to schedule the band's tours around those dates. That's OK, because on the tour bus with him are his wife of 16 years, Melanie, and children, John Michael, 8, Reagan, 6, and Zoe, 3. They go wherever he goes. He wouldn't have it any other way.

TIM LUKE

Tim Luke serves alongside Mark Hall as the adult pastor at Eagle's Landing First Baptist Church. He joined the church staff in March of 2000 after serving as editor of *In Touch* magazine, the devotional magazine of Dr. Charles Stanley's ministry. The former journalist worked as a sportswriter for 10 years, the last four covering the Atlanta Braves. He has been married to Karen for 17 years and has two sons, Jacob, 9, and J.P., 6.

YOU'VE READ THE STORIES.
NOW HEAR THE MUSIC.

NOW AVAILABLE FROM CASTING CROWNS

CASTING CROWNS
INCLUDES "IF WE ARE THE BODY," "WHO AM I" AND "VOICE OF TRUTH"

LIVE FROM ATLANTA
2-DISC CD/DVD SET INCLUDING LIVE CONCERT FOOTAGE FROM THE DEBUT ALBUM AND THE "AMERICAN DREAM" MUSIC VIDEO

LIFESONG
INCLUDES "LIFESONG," "PRAISE YOU IN THIS STORM" AND "DOES ANYBODY HEAR HER"

LIFESONG LIVE
2-DISC CD/DVD SET INCLUDING LIVE CONCE FOOTAGE FROM THE LIFESONG ALBUM AND THE "DOES ANYBOD HEAR HER" MUSIC VIDEC
AVAILABLE 10/3/06